Building Collective Leadership for

Culture Change

The first volume in the series

Publicly Engaged Scholars: Identities, Purposes, Practices

Edited by Anna Sims Bartel, Debra Ann Castillo, and Scott Peters

A list of titles in this series is available at cornellpress.cornell.edu.

Building Collective Leadership for Culture Change

Stories of Relational Organizing on Campus and Beyond

Maria Avila

With Aixle Aman Rivera, Joanna B. Perez,
Alan P. Knoerr, Kathleen Tornow Chai, and
Philip A. Vieira
Foreword by George J. Sánchez

Cornell University Press

Ithaca and London

Copyright © 2023 by Cornell University

All rights reserved. Except for brief quotations in a review, this book, or parts thereof, must not be reproduced in any form without permission in writing from the publisher. For information, address Cornell University Press, Sage House, 512 East State Street, Ithaca, New York 14850. Visit our website at cornellpress.cornell.edu.

First published 2023 by Cornell University Press

Library of Congress Cataloging-in-Publication Data

Names: Avila, Maria, 1955–, author. | Rivera, Aixle Aman, author. | Perez, Joanna B., author. | Knoerr, Alan P., 1957–, author. | Chai, Kathleen Tornow, author. | Vieira, Philip A., author.

Title: Building collective leadership for culture change : stories of relational organizing on campus and beyond / Maria Avila, with Aixle Aman Rivera, Joanna B. Perez, Alan P. Knoerr, Kathleen Tornow Chai, and Philip A. Vieira.

Description: Ithaca : Cornell University Press, 2023. | Series: Publicly engaged scholars: identities, purposes, practices | Includes bibliographical references and index.

Identifiers: LCCN 2022026125 (print) | LCCN 2022026126 (ebook) | ISBN 9781501768705 (hardcover) | ISBN 9781501768712 (paperback) | ISBN 9781501768736 (pdf) | ISBN 9781501768729 (epub)

Subjects: LCSH: Community organization. | Community-based research. | Social change. | Social participation.

Classification: LCC HM766 .A84 2023 (print) | LCC HM766 (ebook) | DDC 361.8—dc23/eng/20220608

LC record available at https://lccn.loc.gov/2022026125

LC ebook record available at https://lccn.loc.gov/2022026126

With love and gratitude *(con amor y agradecimiento)*:

To my husband Dave, for his loving and kind heart. *A mis sobrinas Diana y Paty y sus hijos e hijas Fernando (en memoria y recordándole siempre), Itxayana, Paulina, y Alitzel, por su cariño incondicional. A los líderes y las lideresas, heroínas y héroes en mi familia cuyas enseñanzas son mi guía e inspiración.*

Contents

Foreword by George J. Sánchez   ix

Acknowledgments   xiii

Introduction: Writing Collaboratively, Challenging the Norm   1
Maria Avila

1 Purpose and Overview   6
   Maria Avila

2 Building Collective Leadership through Research in Action and Narrative Inquiry   29
   Maria Avila

3 Discovering Collaborative Research in Action   43
   Kathleen Tornow Chai and Enrique Ortega

4 Igniting a Culture of Relationships and Collective Power in an Elected Office   62
   Aixle Aman Rivera and Ray López-Chang

5 Regional Organizing for Culture Change   83
   Alan P. Knoerr, Celestina Castillo, George J. Sánchez, and Rissi Zimmermann

6 Reimagining Civic Engagement and Academia   112
Joanna B. Perez and Sarah R. Taylor

7 Integrating Civic Engagement into General Education at California State University, Dominguez Hills   138
Philip A. Vieira, Xuefei Deng, and Gabrielle Seiwert

Conclusion: Discoveries and Revelations, Dreaming of Possibilities   160
Maria Avila

Afterword by Alexis Moreno   185

Glossary of Terms and Concepts   191

Bibliography   195

Index   199

Foreword

This book is a testament to the incredible "force of nature" that Maria Avila is in the halls of academia. I, along with every one of the coauthors in this work, can speak to the incredible way that Maria has affected our approach to our own work, from our research to our teaching to the rather mundane aspects of our day-to-day interactions with colleagues and other community members. What she brings to the table is a unique background as an academic, incredible training as an organizer, and immense passion toward making social change happen in every community she encounters.

Maria's background as an immigrant child in a large complex family and an international scholar who crossed the border for parts of her education and work life means that she is an acute observer of the human condition across many cultures, someone who is a deep listener and critical thinker on issues of equity in society. She also attracts individuals to her commitment to social change who are interested in not only sharing aspects of their own culture but also pushing past their own positionalities to work effectively with others. Every one of the chapters of this book is rife with stories of academics and community members looking for alternative ways of making a difference. Maria especially has been able to attract people of color to her academic and community work who see the possibility of a different way of approaching collective action for the common good.

While the personal is always there in these stories, so is the commitment to find new ways to engage in collaborative work in our institutions. Academia has so often adopted a corporate model of engagement, full of rewards for individual accomplishment but with little attention paid to those who remain committed to students or community. What Maria brings to these chapters is a renewed commitment to the relational, something learned in her training as a community organizer who had to earn the trust of those skeptical of people with positions and power. Rather than a series of transactional relationships where the product is valued above everything else, the coauthors of this volume all speak to the building of long-term relationships with colleagues and partners as critical to effective community engagement and collaborative cultural change as critical to their work.

Indeed, one can see Maria's own growth as an academic in these pages, as she gains confidence that her background as an organizer does have a critical role to play at California State University, Dominguez Hills and beyond. Her initial recognition that academic institutions produce siloed work that force her colleagues to work separately is met with new approaches to encourage collaborative work in each of the projects described here. Indeed, the honesty reflected in this learning process as a professor is exhilarating for me, something that is rare in academic books and almost never acknowledged as part of our learning process. Rather than take academia for what is offered and adjust, Maria goes about trying to change the institutional culture and finding colleagues with similar frustrations to collaborate with.

It is important to note that her collaborators were almost always seasoned professionals in various aspects of community engagement themselves even before Maria came on the scene. The tools of one-on-one meetings and shared leadership that she brought from Industrial Areas Foundation organizing were important reminders of the need to engage in thoughtful practice in any community setting, including the highly individualistic realm of academic work. In almost all these projects, the tools served to weather the recent challenges of the pandemic and enhance the anti-racist work that engulfed academic institutions in the wake of the killing of George Floyd. As we move forward in time, clearly these forms of listening and working collaboratively will be needed to make a successful transition back to in-person learning and bringing the lessons of equity and difference to bear in twenty-first-century institutions of higher education.

That the coauthors of these pieces were also willing to write collaboratively to produce their chapters is a sign that the spirit of experimentation and intellectual growth continues to characterize the communities that Maria has played a part in building. Their collective commitments to research in action and to narrative inquiry as processes for developing new insights and breakthroughs in community engagement are important stories for the academic world represented as readers of these pages. The power of stories that are reflected in these processes of learning and collaboration are instructive to the wider world that there is a broad variety of methods that can productively be engaged in academic research and writing.

More than anything else, the belief in collective leadership marks the sophistication of Maria Avila's approach to collaborative thinking and action. Steeped in a world of hierarchical notions of leadership, Maria's approach is a welcome addition to the discussions of how to enact constructive change in communities in academia and in politics. That these methods of collective leadership are critical to culture change in our institutions speaks to the power of these approaches. But commitments to collective leadership also provides a window into what we need today to reestablish a culture of democracy in our society. Recent moves toward totalitarianism and threats to our collective democracy are products of the ways in which our own institutions, including those in higher education, have moved away from practicing democracy and collective governance. My hope is that readers will take the lessons learned in this volume to heart and renew our commitment to democratic practice and long-term relational thinking in all of the institutions that matter in society.

George J. Sánchez, Professor of American Studies
and Ethnicity, University of Southern California

Acknowledgments

Writing a book is a multilayer, multiphase project. This can make it hard to acknowledge everyone who contributed to the various stages of the final product. The deeply collaborative nature of this book makes it easier for me to start by naming and thanking those who responded to my invitation to join me in this very exciting and energizing adventure of using a counter-culture approach to the more common way of writing academic books: writing with those who participate in our research, not about them. I will forever be grateful to those who coauthored the chapters in this book that address the research projects in which they participated: Kathleen Tornow Chai, Enrique Ortega, Aixle Aman Rivera, Ray López-Chang, Alan P. Knoerr, Celestina Castillo, George J. Sánchez, Rissi Zimmermann, Joanna B. Perez, Sarah R. Taylor, Philip A. Vieira, Xuefei Deng, and Gabrielle Seiwert. And of course, I am grateful too to everyone who took part in the five projects but were unable to contribute to the project chapters. They are too many to mention all by name here. I do, however, feel compelled to acknowledge three people. Felipe Ocampo is a former student from the first class I taught in the MSW program at California State University, Dominguez Hills (CSUDH). At the time of the project described in chapter 3 he had graduated and joined the project as a community partner. Andy Florimon, who has also graduated, joined this same project while they were a student in my critical race studies class. Felipe and Andy continued participating in my work even after this project had ended. Adriana Aldana, a faculty member of my department, also participated in this project and along with Andy and Felipe continued collaborating in my research after this project ended.

Alexis Moreno, who wrote the afterword, was not part of the five projects in this book, but she has been a very insightful and valuable thought partner for over a decade, and she was kind enough to read early (and very rough) chapters of this book. Her feedback on these early drafts made a significant contribution to the concept of culture change from her perspective as an experienced community-based professional and researcher.

As always, I must acknowledge my writing mentor, coach, and "partner-in-crime" Scott Peters, whose keen and unusual understanding of my work (not an easy feat!) and his commitment to learning through story has made it possible for me to translate my narrative and the things I have learned through experience (a.k.a tacit knowledge) into academic research and writing. He read and listened to my very early initial thoughts about writing with my research participants, and in the usual way he has done in the past, he challenged me and asked hard questions while at the same time offering supportive guidance and words of encouragement.

As luck or serendipity (or star-alignment?) would have it, as rough drafts became more developed, Scott shared with me that he and two Cornell colleagues were proposing a new book series to Cornell University Press, and he thought my book would fit within the series. I am grateful for this timing, and to his colleagues and coeditors Anna Sims Bartel and Debra Ann Castillo for their feedback in various stages of the manuscript. As the series name

(Publicly Engaged Scholars: Identities, Purposes, Practices) shows, Scott was right about my book's alignment with the series.

There are many other people who were, in different ways, supportive of my five research projects in this book, including the following colleagues at CSUDH:

Kara Dellaccioppa, through her role as director of the Faculty Development Center a few years ago, sponsored a faculty learning community focused on Imagining America, which became one of the projects in this book (chapter 6). This project was also supported by provost Michael Spagna, who provided funds for course release for me and stipends for all other faculty participants. He also provided ongoing support and mentorship through my tenure process. CSUDH dean of undergraduate studies Kimberly Costino was a key financial and strategic supporter of the Faculty Learning Community (FLC) that resulted in creating a civic engagement minor integrated with general education (chapter 7). In her, I found someone who understands and appreciates my work, and she was therefore a great thought partner in this FLC. This project was also financially supported by Cheryl McNight, director of the Center for Service Learning, Internships, and Civic Engagement. Mekada Graham, in her role as chair, offered consistent and ongoing support and encouragement while working on my first project at CSUDH (chapter 3). She also lent an attentive ear any time I needed to think out loud about the overall concept of this book. The three projects I was able to complete at CSUDH were possible in part due to my participation in various campus-wide leadership roles, including serving on a committee to assess campus-wide faculty climate. I thank Clare Weber (former associate vice president of faculty affairs and development) who in my second year at CSUDH asked me to collaborate with her on this committee, especially because this introduced me to the CSUDH Academic

Senate. This exposure led to my nomination as chair of the Faculty Policy Committee by then chair Laura Talamante two years later.

Kevin Bott, Tim Eatman, Jamie Hafft, Erica Kohl-Arenas, and Scott Peters have, at various times and in different ways, created a space for my professional and personal development as leaders and administrators at Imagining America from 2012 through the present (2022). Their commitment to my evolving work was instrumental for one of the projects in the book (chapter 5).

The research collaboratives I attended at the Kettering Foundation at the invitation of Derek Barker, and the funds I received, were all instrumental for the first project described in the book (chapter 3).

Mahinder S. Kingra, Cornell's editorial director, was a very supportive and patient guide throughout the entire process of writing this book.

I am deeply indebted to the blind reviewers for their candid, detailed, and always kind and supportive feedback.

And because my organizing is rooted in my work with the Industrial Areas Foundation (IAF), I will forever be grateful to my colleagues and to the many leaders that I worked with and learned so much from, during the ten years I was an IAF organizer. I especially thank Larry Gordon, my former lead organizer and now a good friend, for his feedback and challenging questions after reading an early draft of a document stating the purpose and methodology of the book.

Introduction

WRITING COLLABORATIVELY, CHALLENGING THE NORM

Maria Avila

For the past decade, I have been on a quest to challenge myself to break the academic norm of writing about those who take part in our research, and instead write with them as coauthors and co-researchers. This book gave me the opportunity to write with my research participants as we reflected together about the ways the projects in which they participated built collective leadership and contributed to creating more collaborative and organizing cultures both in our academic institutions and in community, nonacademic organizations. I am fortunate that many of those who participated in five of my research-in-action projects were up to the challenge, and through a reflective, collaborative writing process, they wrote about the projects in which they participated in chapters 3–7. I began this process by meeting with the authors of each chapter to explain my thoughts on writing collaboratively, while also reflecting with them about their experiences in their respective projects. In addition, the first authors of each chapter agreed to take a leading role in coordinating communications, writing, and meetings with their chapter coauthors. These five colleagues communicated with me as needed. This is a different, more in-depth level of writing collaboratively, and therefore it makes sense to list their names on the cover of the book. This multilayer reflective and writing process led to something different than an edited book. To elaborate, while I write the framing and concluding chapters, the rest of the chapters are focused on the specific projects in which the authors participated. They are all connected to my research, and they all used an intentional approach to writing collaboratively.

The authors of the five chapters include faculty and community partners, and their writing includes examples related to students, academic administrators, policy makers, and funders. Participating faculty teach and research in psychology, sociology, information systems, nursing, community health sciences, mathematics, cognitive science, anthropology, and American studies and ethnicity. I teach social work. Several of us have had administrative and other leadership roles in our respective institutions. All faculty members are tenured; four of us were untenured when we began writing this book. Through our diversity of disciplines, we all make reference to our own particular inquiry methods, our teaching pedagogies, and our community engagement definitions and approaches. Participating community partners work or have worked in not-for-profit organizations related to education, electoral politics, policy, social services, and parent and student organizing. We are diverse in other ways too, including gender, race, nationality, and age, and regarding the populations we work with as faculty and as community partners.

Relevant to the narrative inquiry methodology of this book, all chapters include personal and professional stories. The five chapters also discuss specific skills and practices participants used and/or developed in the projects in which they participated, as well as stories about the authors' work and experience, such as creating a culture of organizing in a school board district (chapter 4); integrating community engagement in their anthropology and sociology classes (chapter 6); participating in a national project focusing on math as a social justice issue (chapter 5); creating a civic engagement minor integrated into general education (chapter 7); creating a student-based organization at a research institution to counter the feeling of isolation and lack of community (chapter 5); creating a community partnership project that led to creating a community-based museum (chapter 5); learning how to work collaboratively with different stakeholders including students, faculty, administrators, and community partners (chapters 3 and 7); learning how to integrate personal and professional narratives in their teaching and research (chapter 3), and taking lessons learned about being collaborative to other areas of their work (chapters 3 and 7). All five chapters relate work experiences about shifting from in-person to online delivery due to the COVID-19 pandemic, and about the ways in which the anti-racist movement that took force in the summer of 2020 influenced their work.

When we began working on this book, all of us were aware that we were engaging in a process that was to unveil itself to us as inquiry, even as we may have asked ourselves at various points of our collaborative reflections and writings whether we would end up with a finished product. And if we did, we wondered, what would it look like? We were also fully aware that this is not the "usual" way in which books are written. Most of us had published before, and some of us have collaborated with other academic colleagues on research projects and in the writing of the findings. None of us had engaged in reflective, collaborative writing as inquiry.

If you are reading this introduction, I invite you to read this book with awareness and openness to what might feel different or foreign compared to other academic publications you may be more familiar and perhaps more comfortable with. Maybe the stories we share here will resonate with your work in some way.

Maybe they will inspire you to build collective leadership to create culture change where you work. Our hope is that what we share in this book will be helpful to you and applicable to your own contexts.

With this brief introduction to the book and the broad range of diversity and backgrounds from those participating in this book, we hope to reach out to an equally broad and diverse audience. This book is for you if you are:

- Faculty teaching research methodologies and movement building–related courses in several disciplines, including education, sociology, urban studies, social policy, social welfare, mathematics, and public health.
- Faculty interested in cocreating reciprocal and mutually beneficial community partnerships through your teaching and/or research.
- Faculty and civic/community engagement–related staff interested in building multi-stakeholder collaborative spaces for collective leadership on your campus.
- Academic administrators interested in supporting community-engaged scholarship, and in working with different stakeholders to build more collaborative cultures on your campus.
- Community organization or school leaders interested in reaching out to faculty and administrators for reciprocal and mutually beneficial partnerships.
- Leaders/staff of faculty development–related centers or offices interested in cocreating more relevant faculty and student-related programming.
- Undergraduate or graduate students interested in learning about collaborative and action research methodologies and applying them to your research projects.
- Interested in diversity and equity-related work on your campuses or community organizations.
- Philanthropists interested in finding ways to build reciprocal, mutually beneficial relationships with your grantees.

- Government-related leaders looking for ways to increase collaborative, action-oriented relationships with your constituency.
- Hungry and open to collaborative facilitation approaches as teachers, or as workshop or meeting facilitators.
- Interested in joining or creating a movement to create more collaborative and humane cultures in academia and in community organizations.

Finally, the approach offered here is relevant for academics and nonacademics concerned about the state of our democratic society and the level and quality of democratic participation in our institutions, organizations, and society at large in the United States and in many other countries.

1

Purpose and Overview

Maria Avila

> Kêytê-aya [as used by the Cree Elders] teach us that it is important to begin any process by acknowledging our place of knowing and identifying who we are and our purpose.
> —Cindy Hanson, Chantelle Renwick, José Sousa, and Angelina Weenie

I am often inspired by the teachings of indigenous communities, perhaps first ignited by one such teaching I had in Mexico as a student of social work. My classmates and I took a field trip to the mountains in the state of Chihuahua where the Tarahumara Indians live. Although too young then to fully comprehend the significance of this experience, I do remember a myriad of conflicting feelings while being at a Catholic mass conducted fully in the Tarahumara language and not understanding a word of it. Then I tried to mix and mingle afterward, only to realize no one seemed to want to talk to me. I did not know if they did not speak Spanish or if they just did not want to talk to me. I was a foreigner in my own country. This is when I first became aware of the privileges I enjoyed as a "mestiza" (of Spanish and Indigenous descent). In the United States, my awareness and education about American Indians and Indigenous peoples of the world has evolved through the years, and with it, an appreciation for indigenous traditions and types of wisdom.

The quote above is about the Cree people in Canada, and it inspires me to start this introduction by sharing my narrative.[1] In what follows, I share parts of my story to illustrate the origins of my leadership and social justice interest, as well as my civically engaged scholarship and methodology. In doing this, I am honoring the teachings of the Cree Elders of starting every project and meeting by acknowledging our purpose, our place of knowing, and who we are.

My Family Roots

I was born and raised in the state of Chihuahua, in the northern part of Mexico. I am one of thirteen children, and the youngest of eleven women. I had a peculiar place in my family because the youngest of all thirteen children is the second of only two males. There were several women between the first and the second male. My youngest brother was therefore received with a great deal of excitement. Being the youngest of eleven women did not have much relevance at this point. My father was an agricultural worker most of his life. Neither my father or my mother finished grammar school (my father could read and write a little, my mother could only spell her name). They were responsible and loving parents, and they did what they could to figure out how to support their growing family, even if this meant moving their family around looking for work. I was five the first time my family moved from a small city to an even smaller, rural town. By the time I was a teenager, we had moved four times. One of these moves was caused, I am told, by politics. As the story goes, my father had gotten involved in the elections for the town's mayor, and his candidate lost.

The town was small, and political divisions carried all kinds of consequences, including life and death.

Our narratives evolve throughout life. When we pause to reflect about our lives, often we are not fully aware of what part of our story is going to surface at any given point. The story I just related about my father came to me at this particular moment. Stories have both clear and hidden meanings, or at least meanings not fully discovered yet. When I was a community organizer during the 1990s, I was often asked why I did this work. For a long time, I did not know how to answer. My father's story is giving new meaning to this question: both my father's involvement in politics and my family's many moves in search of work. My older siblings have stories of many other times when my family moved before I was born. Ever since I came to the United States in 1981, I have been asked many, many times how it is that I have done so many things in my life. Implicitly or explicitly, this question seems to be about my professional accomplishments given my family background. Who knows what the answer is? In all honesty, the answer to this question is not very interesting to me. What is interesting to me is the process of discovery I experience every time I reflect on and share different parts of my story.

My Academic Roots

My community organizing experiences began with my practicum as a social work student in Ciudad Juárez in the 1970s. Yet much of my civically engaged scholarship comes from my ten years as an organizer with the Industrial Areas Foundation (IAF) from 1990 to 2000 in Albuquerque, New Mexico; South Central Los Angeles (currently referred to as South LA); and Northern California. To me, my organizing experiences have been, and continue to be, clear and powerful sources of knowledge and inspiration. Organizing is how I first learned about the importance of collective leadership to create long-lasting social change. I also learned that collective leadership is built through relational, one-on-one, and house meetings.

In the IAF model of organizing, every campaign we embarked on was preceded by numerous one-on-one meetings and house meetings, where issues of interest and potential leaders were identified. These meetings were then followed by research on those issues, conducted by organizers and leaders (IAF church/organization members) before deciding on strategies and actions to take. This process informed the focus of the campaign and determined who we could approach that had the power and/or resources to achieve our organizing goals and create change. These organizing steps have a significant connection with my current research methodologies of research in action and narrative inquiry. This realization came to me first during my doctoral research in Ireland, and it has become clearer through my development as a civically engaged scholar. I will elaborate more on my research methodologies in the next chapter. At this point, I want to further illustrate the organizing process by sharing a memory from my organizing years with IAF. I have flashbacks about these events, even decades later. I frame the narrative, first, with how I found my way to IAF.

The story I am reflecting about in the context of this book begins in the early 1990s, in my early years with IAF. At the end of 1990, I had moved from Los Angeles to Albuquerque in part to explore whether I could find my way back to organizing, about a decade after I came to the United States. I had tried social work and adult education–related jobs in Chicago and Los Angeles but found myself missing the organizing work I had started in Ciudad Juárez in the 1970s. My early work experiences in the United

States taught me that organizing was not relevant in social work or adult education. It was in Albuquerque that I learned about the IAF work in El Paso, Texas, and about IAF's national ten-day training. After visiting the IAF organization in El Paso and attending IAF training, I began the groundwork to create an IAF organization in Albuquerque. Once this organization was on its way, I moved back to Los Angeles (LA), where I started working for IAF in South Central LA in 1992. I began meeting with IAF leaders from member churches and identifying key leaders within those churches, which often included the pastors and those with whom they worked closely. Through these meetings I heard stories about issues of importance to them and others in their churches, and about past and current efforts to tackle such issues. This is how I found myself organizing around the need for a grocery store in a South Central community surrounding a Catholic church, not far from the University of Southern California (USC).

The parishioners of this church were mostly recent immigrants from Latin America, many of whom did not own cars and spoke little or no English. There were no large grocery stores within walking distance, and families had to do their shopping for essential groceries at small neighborhood stores that often focused on selling liquor. Many of the church members were mothers with small children. These women told me that they had to take the bus to the nearest grocery store about five miles away, where they could find all their groceries at better prices but then had to struggle to carry the groceries home while also attending to their accompanying children. These recent immigrant families were learning about life in the United States while raising young children and working long hours often in multiple jobs, which did not always pay minimum wage nor provide health insurance. I learned all this through one-on-one meetings with church members, sometimes while visiting them at their homes, other times at church after mass over *pan dulce* (Mexican pastry) and coffee.

In addition to the sale of liquor being the main focus of the small stores in the neighborhood, their products were overpriced, as they had to compete with large grocery chains. These stores were also not the safest places for families, as they were often surrounded by people who bought liquor and drank it outside of the stores. The neighborhoods where this organizing campaign was taking place had another challenge to contend with: USC had begun expanding, which was bringing up surrounding property values and making it more difficult for working families to afford their apartments' rent. At the time, the demographics of South Central LA were shifting from African American to Latino, working-class families. Many African American families were moving to cities where they could afford to buy a home and where they felt it would be safe to raise their families; they then had to often commute an hour or longer to jobs in LA. These demographic changes were reflected everywhere in South Central LA, and churches were no exception.

After conducting a number of one-on-ones and identifying some members who had leadership potential as well as the self-interest to motivate them to take leading roles in an organizing campaign, I began meeting with them and with the pastor as a group. In these meetings we discussed elements we needed to research, such as whether there were large grocery chains who would be interested in opening a store in the area, who in their management team would be the right person to approach for a meeting, and which elected officials represented the area. While most church members were recent immigrants and therefore new to the neighborhood, there were a small number of parishioners who had lived in the community and attended the church for many years. These parishioners were ethnically mixed. Through one-on-ones with them

I learned that an empty lot across from the church had been considered as a possible location for a grocery store for many years, but for different reasons the organizing for this to happen had not been sustained.

All this information helped us make an analysis of power dynamics and potential alliances, as well as explore organizing tactics. We then built on this information by researching what we could about whether it would be in the self-interest of major grocery chains and elected officials to build such a store. These were our main research questions, although we did not think of it as research as defined by academia. We simply viewed this as organizing practices. Based on findings from our research, we proceeded to put together an organizing campaign that would include meetings with the management of one major grocery store chain and with the city council representative of the area. It also included identifying leaders who would be able to make these meetings happen. With the basics of our organizing campaign, we called all church members to a meeting where we shared our campaign and some of the stories I had heard through my one-on-one meetings. We had them break into small groups to discuss whether this campaign made sense to them, share questions or concerns they had, and determine whether they thought they would be able to attend future meetings and actions that would evolve as the campaign got going.

My telling of this story now may read as if every step was clear to me, and almost mechanical. But even as I write about it now, my heart beats remembering moments of uncertainty and anxiety. Would I be able to help those leaders prepare for their meetings with people in power? Would I be able to meet with people in power? What if the campaign did not succeed? I was, after all, still developing my organizing skills and mindset in the context of IAF's power-focused, broad-based, collective leadership organizing model.

Years after this campaign began, and after I had moved on to organize in Northern California, a major chain grocery store was built. It took numerous meetings with elected officials and grocery chain executives, marches, prayers, flyers, and talks at Sunday masses. One particular march comes to mind. My mother, at the time almost eighty, was visiting from Ciudad Juárez and was with me that day. About a hundred or so church members and IAF leaders and pastors from other churches marched around the lot across the church, which we had identified as the location for the store. We had created signs that communicated the purpose of our march. We chanted and gave speeches. My mother didn't march with us but watched from a distance. I kept an eye on her while guiding leaders on their specific roles and speeches. Her face looked perplexed, but in a good way. It seemed to glow with pride, but maybe not so much for my organizing role. My mother, and really most of my family, have never quite understood what I do for a living. My mother was a devoted Catholic all her life. In fact, during the last five years of her life, while suffering from Alzheimer's, bedridden, and unable to recognize any of her children or pray, she would still give thanks to *Diosito y la Virgencita* (God and the Virgin) for another day of life. What made my mother's face glow with pride that day was seeing her daughter marching in front of a Catholic church and surrounded by so many priests! This part of my job she understood, and every time she had an opportunity to see me interacting with priests it brought her happiness and pride.

Collective Leadership

Building leadership is contextual. My organizing experiences outside of academia are still relevant to me, with some adjustments for context. For this reason, I offer another story from my

IAF organizing to share lessons about the steps in building collective leadership, which are also relevant to the five research projects offered in later chapters. These projects are examples of my organizing experiences in academia and with my community partners, and they are all underpinned by community organizing practices that aim to create institutional and community culture change.[2]

Organizing campaigns like the one about building the grocery store is one example of IAF events where leaders practice and develop. IAF also organizes large events (or actions in IAF language) where institutional and organizational members (leaders in IAF language) demand resources and recognition from elected officials and others in positions of power. These events are usually attended by thousands of IAF members from the various member institutions, and they involve singing, prayer, and story sharing. A significant purpose of these actions, however, is to have an arena where members can practice the leadership and organizing skills they are learning, to recognize and practice their own power, and to then reflect together about the experience to continue learning and developing as leaders. In other words, those actions, even in cases when resources are gained for the communities involved, would not be as relevant if there are no leaders in formation who can then transform dominant power structures.

Prior to the day of the large action, IAF member institutions in a specific region embark on a process similar to the one I described about building the grocery store.[3] This process is how issues people care about emerge, along with research on those issues and who has the power to deliver on such issues. This is also how collective leadership and relational power is built. By the day of the action, representatives from each institution are well aware of what is at stake and what their specific roles at the action will be. The action is immediately followed by an evaluation, undertaken with the main leaders who were part of the process leading to the action, of what was gained or not and what further organizing steps are needed. Most importantly, this is an opportunity to recognize leaders who engaged on the stage (literally) with those in power (often elected officials and/or business leaders), those who delivered leaders from their institutions, and anyone else who had a role in the action.

Stories tend to illustrate best. One of the leaders I remember the most is Imelda (pseudonym). An immigrant from Mexico, she did not have much schooling and spoke very little English. Imelda's family lived in a rental apartment, and she and her husband worked multiple jobs to make ends meet. Through leadership trainings, lifting her narrative, and individual mentoring, Imelda became a leader in a campaign for affordable housing. She had an incredible contagious energy and thirst for justice. What I most remember about her is that while briefing her about roles she would play in specific actions, and then debriefing with her after, her eyes lit up and seemed to get bigger with sharp attention, all the while showing a wide smile. She would also crack a joke or two to illustrate what she was hearing and learning. I was laughing and learning with her. People like her are often described as "ordinary" people. This means they are not supposed to meet face to face with people with more education, power, and resources than they have. Yet this is exactly what Imelda did, as she stood on a large stage, demanding a clear commitment from elected officials to invest in affordable housing for her community. She had an interpreter, given her language skills and the language skills of those on the stage she was facing. You would think this would have made her nervous, and possibly make her change her mind about her charge last minute. But no. With a firm voice and demeanor, she stood tall, pausing for translation in between statements, and then demanding a firm and clear answer. Imelda was also one of the leaders in her Catholic church doing one-on-one and house meetings to learn about people's interests and motivations to organize, listening to their stories and sharing her own, often over a meal at her house or theirs. This is how she built the collective of leaders who trusted her enough to respond to her call to attend the housing action.

This approach to building collective leadership and relational power to create change is at the core of my training in IAF's model of organizing. The context in which I currently work is no doubt different, and yet, with relevant adjustments, this approach has been very similar to the way I build spaces for collective leadership to emerge, in academia and with my community partners. I used parts of this model to guide my work at Occidental's Center for Community Based Learning, and throughout my doctoral and postdoctoral research.

One advantage I have as an academic that I did not have as an IAF organizer is that I do not feel pressure to recruit member institutions or leaders. I have the luxury of using my values and organizing skills through research, which affords me a great deal of space to let the process of building leadership and identifying action items evolve, while learning with those in the collaborative spaces I create. Of course, I have other demands, such as producing enough research and publications while teaching and doing many other departmental and university tasks. If I can identify internal or external grants (and this is no easy task) to sponsor my research projects, I can focus more on exploring ways to create culture change, and less on creating massive, immediate change in the university or in surrounding communities. My aspiration is that through these explorations we can build interest and momentum in processes that collectively cocreate new and effective ways to enhance democratic, collaborative ways of being. At the moment, this is not an aspiration I sense many of my colleagues

Purpose and Overview 17

and community partners share, hence the purpose of my work. There are other models and concepts of leadership development I find useful for my current academic context, which merge naturally with community organizing concepts.

A concept I see in close alignment with leadership and with organizing in general is civic agency, and it is something I believe we all have access to, but we are not always intentional about how we use it. KerryAnn O'Meara offers an academic perspective about civic agency and its use. Her perspective is based on a study about the extent to which civically engaged faculty practice civic agency. She writes that "civic agency allows one to pursue goals that matter to them via intentional strategies and capacities, both learned and innate."[4] She explains that for the purpose of the study she focused on faculty who were able to effectively recognize and navigate through institutional barriers while integrating civically engaged pedagogies in their classrooms and in their field. O'Meara's concept of civic agency is helpful as an element in a process of building collaborative civic agency through collective leadership, and it has significant resonance with my IAF story above.

As I continue to learn from my research collaborative projects, concepts of leadership that offer what I consider more wholistic, less traditional or mainstream models of leadership resonate with me. I have developed an interest in looking for counterculture methods that shift our current paradigms as we face overwhelming world problems. Chellie Spiller, Maunganui Wolfgramm, Ella Henry, and Robert Pouwhare, for example, challenge us to look at collective leadership as a paradigm that indigenous communities have practiced for millennia. Through what to me feels like an admonishing tone (and a welcomed one), they urge us to recognize that those who see collective leadership as something new are ignoring the contributions of ancient practices and wisdom such as this. They share with us an ecosystems concept of leadership as "a revolutionary departure from more traditional scholarship, not just on leadership but also collective leadership, because of the extraordinary set of relationships it encompasses, including those across generations and across living and nonliving entities."[5] The inclusion of relationships across generations and with living and nonliving things is clearly a radical departure from contemporary concepts that focus primarily on leadership as it applies to institutional, community, and societal contexts in the here and now, and with relevance to living, human beings. This also challenges the current, predominant academic discourse around "evidence-based" practice and "data-driven" decisions, especially because this notion implies that evidence and data only apply to academic, empirical research, denying the multitude types of evidence that come from nonacademic ways of knowing.

The approach shared in this book, although not completely aligned with the ecosystems concept of leadership described above, is different from what most current civic engagement models use, in and outside of higher education. Most civic engagement models tend to be based on civically engaged courses and cocurricular student service (in academia), and on short-term or issue-specific projects (outside of academia). In my experience working in the not-for-profit sector and from recent accounts from community partners and funders, community organizations may want to collaborate on common issues to better serve their constituencies, but they often face a number of barriers, such as competing for funding and constituencies. My experience as a community organizer inside and outside of academia has taught me that long-term sustainable change requires a collective of people who are interested in creating change, to allow and trust a process that involves defining what this means for them and their communities or institutions. This process also involves learning and practicing the skills to become active members of the public spaces where we work and live. Our fragmented, product-oriented, often disengaged democratic society does not offer many opportunities to do this. Creating these spaces is an important driver for the approach I present with my partners in this book, especially through the five chapters my partners author, where they share their reflections about the projects in which they participated. These five projects are underpinned by collaborative research in action, narrative inquiry, and community organizing. This, in brief, means that we all learned together as the projects evolved, that we learned through sharing stories about ourselves and about our work, and that I used community organizing practices to build collective leadership and move us to specific goals and actions. I elaborate on these methodologies in the next chapter.

In this approach to building collective leadership, these are the steps I follow as an organizer, though not necessarily in this order:

- Conducting relational one-on-one meetings with people I think might be interested in my work, to learn about people's self-interest through sharing personal and/or professional stories.
- Inviting those for whom my work resonates to projects I am working on, based on their interests.
- Sharing my aim to build collaborative spaces where we can share personal and professional stories, learn together, identify specific goals/actions together, reflect on and assess our accomplishments together, and frame all this with participatory research in action and narrative inquiry.
- Sharing my organizing approach that aims to build collective leadership to create culture change in our institutions and communities related to disconnectedness, individualism, and

hyperactivity, and to build reciprocal, mutually beneficial, long-lasting civically engaged partnerships.
- Offering a space to share reading discussions related to participatory research in action, narrative inquiry, community organizing, and civically engaged scholarship.

This type of organizing is different from community organizing we are all most familiar with, which is usually not related to organizing in higher education and/or in our institutions. My approach to organizing is based on a sense of urgency to create and recreate collaborative spaces where we can grow and harvest democratic practices essential to tackling the overwhelming issues we are facing worldwide. With this approach I operate under the assumption that unless we counter our individualistic and hyperactive culture and do this together in collectives of leaders, we will, at best, continue to compete with each other for resources and constituents for the myriad of issues we each care about. At worst, we will be paralyzed by the daunting work needed to create long-term sustainable change. Many of us are already in either of these two categories.

While the projects I am bringing to this book will be discussed in chapters 3 through 7, let me briefly introduce them here. I will use the authors' full names for easy reference with the chapters. I will, however, refer to them by their first names when I introduce the authors in each chapter, and in the concluding chapter because this helps me feel a warmer, relational connection with them. In the first project (chapter 3), Kathleen Tornow Chai and Enrique Ortega discussed whether their disciplinary research and teaching methodologies were adequate for engaging with community in reciprocal and democratic ways. They struggled, for example, with the participatory research and narrative inquiry that I introduced in this project, this being the first time they were exposed to these methodologies. The chapter about this project describes this tension and how the authors resolved it, illustrating so with their own narratives. In the second project (chapter 4), Aixle Aman Rivera and Ray López-Chang give their perspective about this project as staff members in a newly elected school board member's office. They share how they and their colleagues in this office were challenged by the limitations of a culture typical of most elected officials' offices, where field staff are reactive to their constituents' needs. They describe their own transformation from service providers to community organizers. In the third project (chapter 5), Alan P. Knoerr, Celestina Castillo, George J. Sánchez, and Rissi Zimmermann write about their experiences as members of the Imagining America Southern California regional cluster in the Los Angeles metropolitan area, with participants from higher education and community organizations. The authors use collaborative writing to reflect about the role of community organizing in this project and ways in which they and their institutions and organizations have benefited from this project. In their chapter, they wrestled with questions related to creating culture change and what this means to each of them in connection to their personal and professional narratives. The fourth project (chapter 6), written by Joanna B. Perez and Sarah R. Taylor, aimed to integrate arts, humanities, and design into courses from various disciplines. While reflecting about the project, the authors found themselves realizing that higher education does not value collaborative work in general, and civically engaged scholarship in particular. The authors of this chapter share their reflections about this and begin to imagine a more collaborative culture in higher education. While the first four projects lasted about a year, the fifth project (chapter 7) met for four semesters. This project was also the first time I was able to integrate the main stakeholders relevant to civically engaged scholarship in a sustained way. These are faculty, community partners, students, and civic engagement departments. This project originated from a request from the dean of undergraduate studies to figure out how to integrate civically engaged scholarship into the general education curriculum, and the dean not only supported the project, but she was also an active participant and part of the cocreative and collaborative learning process. The biggest sources of tension, but perhaps also the most rewarding and educational part of this project, came from figuring out ways to collaborate, learn, and make decisions together across this wide range of stakeholders. In this chapter, Philip A. Vieira, Xuefei Deng, and Gabrielle Seiwert share their deep and provocative reflections about what higher education and other sectors of society might look like if they were to act more collaboratively with all relevant stakeholders.

In all five projects, participants were engaged with me and with each other in a deeply relational, reflective, collaborative, at times challenging process. In all five projects too, there was a feeling that we had done something new, unique, and different. This felt good to me, and it seemed to feel good to the participants. I say "it seemed" based on reactions during meetings, and from final reports where I quoted participants' testimonies regarding what they had learned and experienced, and what we had accomplished in the projects. I get this sense also from the willingness participants have shown in their commitment to make the time to attend meetings. I remember attending a faculty retreat during the time of the first project on my campus and running into two participants who stopped me to remind me of an upcoming meeting as if they were looking forward to it. This was satisfying to me and I saw this as a sign of ownership of the project, especially given that these two participants were very busy with their responsibilities as department chairs, and that they had only known me for less than a year. Participants from the five projects have told me that the collaborative space we created is not found anywhere else in their work. Some have shared similar thoughts in their feedback to the final project reports I wrote.

One could argue that these reports and what I observed in the meetings could be used as evidence that the methodology I used with the five projects was successful in building collective leadership to create culture change. To be honest, I was tempted to do so, thinking I could offer it as an approach to others interested in creating collaboratives in order to build collective leadership and create culture change within their campuses, organizations, or communities. As I embarked on this book, I felt tension about lingering questions that cannot be answered by these reports and my post-project reflections. In truth, I am not able to answer these questions alone. Some questions relate directly to my methodology for building collective leadership through research in action and narrative inquiry, and the extent to which these methodologies combined with community organizing practices can create more collaborative, action-oriented cultures. Other questions stem from the turmoil many of us in the United States (and around the world) experienced personally and professionally starting in 2020, caused by the COVID-19 pandemic and the revitalized anti-racist movement. These are the questions I came with to the collaborative reflective and writing methodology I embarked on in this book:

- In what ways are research in action and narrative inquiry combined with community organizing effective in building collective leadership?
- In what ways did the five projects create culture change?
- Is it possible to change the culture of silos and disconnectedness, both within and outside of academia?

- How did the COVID-19 pandemic and the anti-racist movement influence our sense of what we accomplished through the five projects?
- In what ways might our collaborative writing lead to new opportunities to continue organizing for culture change?

With these questions and curiosity in mind, I felt motivated to reach out to project participants to see if they would be interested in helping me make sense of these questions, and of what really happened in each project. To my delight and surprise, many of them agreed. Given these times of doing everything remotely (2020–21), I engaged in virtual reflection sessions with participants from each of the five projects first, and then met with them personally when this was safe for our health. I then realized I would not be satisfied with writing up our findings on my own, so I invited them to author the chapters relevant to projects in which they participated, based on our reflection meetups and on lessons learned through writing collaboratively. This added to this book project by experimenting with writing as inquiry. My hope is that reflecting and writing together about our collaborative experiences will not only produce good knowledge and lessons tied to a rich, trustworthy understanding of what really happened in the five collaborative projects. My hope is that the process itself will advance the work of building and strengthening relationships and collective leadership, thus advancing my organizing work.

Why We Need Culture Change

Through nearly two decades in the civic engagement field as a practitioner and as a scholar, I have experienced firsthand what many academics have written about: that the culture of academia is a culture of silos.[6] In my experience, this applies to civically engaged faculty as well. This is in part because collaboration in academia, and in civically engaged scholarship in particular, tends not to be valued or rewarded for tenure and promotion.[7] This makes it challenging for faculty to build long-term sustainable, mutually beneficial community partnerships. In such a scenario, it is also challenging to invest in the often labor-intensive demands of civically engaged teaching.

Many scholars have written about the widely shared, aspirational goal to see universities engaged with their surrounding communities with such a level of collaboration and reciprocity. Byron White, for instance, holds that for this type of reciprocal engagement to occur, community partners need to be invited to "the table" by university administration.[8] Randy Stoecker and Elizabeth Tryon argue that community partners' needs should drive engagement with universities, not the other way around.[9] To me this sounds like community partners need to invite university administrators and faculty to their tables. Regardless of who is invited to whose table, actions are likely not taken in spaces where all stakeholders are open to exploring ways to cocreate partnerships through processes based on dialogue, story sharing, and openness to discovering strategies and creating new knowledge together, across different disciplines and stakeholders. Nor do those at the table generally begin by talking about or acknowledging their place of knowing, identifying who they are, and what their purpose is. And building collective leadership is not usually what drives university-community partnerships. This does not mean that the stakeholders in these civic engagement efforts do not believe, at least in principle, in creating such spaces.

I know, for example, that faculty members are part of multiple service committees, as well as research/writing-focused groups within and across disciplines, and some use research practices similar to research in action and to narrative inquiry. I know too that students collaborate with each other through student clubs and group assignments, and community partners form short- and long-term coalitions as needed. I also know many colleagues who use research methodologies similar to mine. What is missing, in my view, is for stakeholders to share their scholarship/work and personal motivations for it, in collaborative spaces where new, interdisciplinary, intersectoral knowledge can emerge, and where collective actions can evolve. This requires trusting relationships, patience, and an openness to the unknown places that being together in this type of space may take us. All this is hard to find in academia, and in society in general. In my view as an organizer and civically engaged scholar, this is at the core of our currently fragmented democratic society, and it prevents us from working together on solving society's problems and the way they affect our institutions, organizations, and communities.

The six years it took me to get tenure at CSUDH allowed me to witness and experience firsthand the culture of hyperactivity in which full-time faculty operate. I know all about the feeling of being always on call for students in and outside the classroom, about the tension created by expectations to publish and to serve on university committees, and to keep up with shared departmental chores. I know too that my students are overextended with school demands that often compete with family and full-time jobs. This is the case of the students attending CSUDH, who are primarily Latino and African American, and the first in their families to attend college. My community partners in the not-for-profit sector and K-12 schools have their own work and life demands, often underfunded and understaffed. One could say that we cannot escape these predicaments. This is just part of life. But we must recognize that whether we place the blame on the effects of decades of neoliberalism-related policies and behaviors, as some of us believe, or to other explanations others may believe in, hyperactivity is often viewed as a sign of success and status. This is highly valued by society and, one could argue, internalized by all of us individually and collectively. The point is that this type of hyperactive culture undermines the approach I am sharing in this book. All this is to say that I am keenly aware of how challenging this approach can be, and how easy and tempting it can feel to not even try. And to some, this might feel like an unrealistic panacea.

We write this book in the context of the unique historical moment we are living through, in the United States and in the world. The political divide in the United States between conservative and progressive politics is at its greatest, at least within the time I have lived in this country. But we are also seeing new windows and glimmers of hope for racial justice. For most of 2020 we were in involuntary lockdown in our homes (even if partial for some of us), forced by the COVID-19 pandemic to heed what to me feels like Nature's clamor for us to let it breathe. My deepest hope is that we may take this momentous opportunity to consider exploring more humane and just ways of being for our sake, our democracy, and for our planet. With all this in mind, as you read through our discoveries and collaborative experiences, I invite you to listen to the Cree Elders and take a moment to acknowledge your place of knowing and identify your purpose and who you are.

Notes

1. Cindy Hanson, Chantelle Renwick, José Sousa, and Angelina Weenie, "Decolonizing and Indigenizing Adult Education," in *Proceedings of the 37th CASAE/ACÉÉA Annual Conference*, ed. Robert McGray and Vera Woloshyn (Regina, SK: University of Regina, 2018), 98–103.

2. I am aware that academic institutions are a form of community, but for the sake of clarity, I am using the word "institutional" to refer to higher education and other institutions or organizations, and the word "community" for communities outside of higher education.

3. The national network is made out of one or more affiliate organizations throughout the country. For example, at the time I was working with IAF, Los Angeles had four organizations within the metropolitan area.

4. KerryAnn O'Meara, *Because I Can: Exploring Faculty Civic Agency*, Kettering Foundation Working Paper 2012-1, https://www.kettering.org/sites/default/files/product-downloads/OMeara-KFWP2012-01-FINAL.pdf.

5. Chellie Spiller, Rachel Maunganui Wolfgramm, Ella Henry, and Robert Pouwhare, "Paradigm Warriors: Advancing a Radical Ecosystems View of Collective Leadership from an Indigenous Māori Perspective," *Human Relations* 73, no. 4 (2019): 516–43. Other readings related to collective leadership include Adrianne Maree Brown, *Emergent Strategy: Shaping Change, Changing World* (Chico, CA: AK Press, 2017); Melanie James, "Emergent Strategy," in *The International Encyclopedia of Strategic Communication*, ed. Robert L. Heath, Winni Johansen, Jesper Falkheimer, Kirk Hallahan, Juliana J. C. Raupp, and Benita Steyn (Hoboken, NJ: John Wiley & Sons, 2018); Gail T. Fairhurst, Brad Jackson, Erica G. Foldy, and Sonia M. Ospina, "Studying Collective Leadership: The Road Ahead," *Human Relations* 73, no. 4 (2020): 598–614; Charlene A. Carruthers, *Unapologetic: A Black, Queer, and Feminist Mandate for Radical Movements* (Boston: Beacon, 2019).

6. Steve Kollowich, "Blasting Academic Silos: American University Officials Say the Insularity of Colleges within Universities Is a Bane to Both I.T. Efficiency and Scholarly Innovation," *Inside Higher Ed*, January 18, 2010, https://www.insidehighered.com/news/2010/01/18/blasting-academic-silos.

7. See, for example, KerryAnn O'Meara, "Encouraging Multiple Forms in Faculty Reward Systems: Does It Make a Difference?" *Research in Higher Education* 46, no. 5 (2005): 479–510; Claire Snyder-Hall, *Civic Aspirations: Why Some Higher Education Faculty Are Reconnecting Their Professional and Public Lives* (Dayton, OH: Kettering Foundation, 2013).

8. Byron White, *Navigating the Power Dynamics between Institutions and Their Communities* (Kettering Foundation, 2009), https://www.kettering.org/sites/default/files/product-downloads/Navigating_Power_Dynamics.pdf.

9. Randy Stoecker and Elizabeth Tryon, *The Unheard Voices: Community Organizations and Service Learning* (Philadelphia: Temple University Press, 2009).

2

Building Collective Leadership through Research in Action and Narrative Inquiry

Maria Avila

As a civically engaged scholar and organizer, I work with others to create a more democratic, collaborative culture in academic institutions where I work, and in the communities with which I partner. My experience in pursuing this work has led me to raise two important questions, related to themes I first raised in chapter 1: Is it possible to change the culture of silos and disconnectedness, both within and outside of academia? If so, how?

These questions are met with a good deal of skepticism, particularly regarding the possibilities for change within the academy. It is widely known that faculty tend to work in isolation, and civically engaged faculty are no exception. When faculty come together, particularly tenure-track faculty, it is often related to university committees, research projects, or grants, through which the depth and the length of their collaboration tends to be limited beyond the specific set goals. Some call these transactional relationships. It is true that many faculty members engage in university committees out of interest to make their institutions a better place for all its stakeholders, and for the surrounding communities. It is also true that many civically engaged faculty often engage with community projects through their teaching and/or research out of a need to find meaning in their careers and/or escape from institutions that do not value them. However, they often have little or no motivation to organize to create a different type of culture within their institutions. This is in part because their civically engaged scholarship is not always valued or rewarded for tenure and promotion.

Valuing and rewarding civically engaged scholarship are important at various levels. First, civically engaged scholarship is crucial for higher education to engage with regional, national, and global communities responsibly, productively, and reciprocally. This is a social and moral mandate, but it is also linked to higher education's credibility in their regions and with different sectors of society. This credibility is linked to student enrollment and with partnerships that can lead to internships and employment for students, and for capital and research investment, among other benefits. However, if civically engaged scholarship is not rewarded for tenure and promotion, faculty engagement with the community may not be based on long-term, sustainable, and mutually beneficial partnerships.

Second, higher education aims (and claims) to have a culture where governance is a practice shared by all its institutional stakeholders. While the typical stakeholders in this context tend to be faculty, students, administrators, and staff, universities have long made claims that community partners should be viewed as stakeholders with a voice in matters of the university.[1] I am hopeful but also skeptical that this role for stakeholders will be reciprocally, jointly cocreated and operationalized. At the moment, faculty are the main stakeholders when it comes to civically engaged scholarship, but also for delivering for the main product universities offer, namely, undergraduate and graduate degrees. If faculty are not feeling valued or recognized, however, it stands to reason that they will be less likely to engage in institutional matters, and less motivated to engage in creating a supportive, more democratic institutional culture.

Third, with the shrinking of public funding for academia, higher education institutions have become more businesslike in the way they are managed, and in their need to secure enough revenue through student enrollment and through large, commercial partnerships to sponsor research and new university buildings. This translates into a culture of competitiveness among faculty, where a huge amount of time and energy are spent in pursuing funding, leaving faculty physically and mentally exhausted, not to mention demoralized.[2] This scenario, which used to exist mainly in large research institutions, is now rapidly taking hold even of state-funded institutions like mine, where teaching used to be the primary function.

From Individual to Collaborative, Civically Engaged Scholarship

What can we do to address these problems? How might we build and sustain a more democratic culture of collaboration to foster collective leadership that enables us to break out of our various silos?

As introduced in the previous chapter, my partners and I (partners in this sense means participants from the five projects, who are authoring chapters of the book) will share five research projects, along with our thoughts and lessons about the extent to which we were able to create a culture of collaboration and collective leadership. The projects we share are all underpinned by community-organizing practices that aim to create institutional and community culture change. The specific aspects of the culture to be changed are contextual. That is, each project's participants identify aspects of their institutional culture they are troubled by and motivated to change. For instance, working with faculty participants who are involved with civic engagement, relevant aspects of the culture that require change often include criteria and systems for assessing and rewarding civically engaged scholarship. Working with community members in the project I led with a Los Angeles school board member's office, the interest was in creating a community organizing culture and learning-related practices to develop parental leadership in the board member's district. Ultimately, all projects aimed to create spaces where participants could engage in conversations that lead to cocreating the ultimate goals of the projects, using the three methodologies I introduced in the previous chapter and others relevant to each context.

As an organizer, my main role in each project was to practice and teach my community organizing skills of relationship building, building collective leadership, strategizing for action based on power dynamics and resources, and ongoing critical reflection. The approach we used is exploratory and experiential, evolving naturally (or organically) based on conversations, interests, and group dynamics during and between meetings. My hope is that this approach will be of interest for anyone motivated to address the fragmented and divided democratic society in which we live, and the ways in which this manifests itself in our institutions and organizations.

As my partners and I reflected on what we experienced through the five projects, we realized that this process of collaboration and cocreation involved periods of uncertainty, but it also built community and eventually led to specific and concrete actions. Paramount in the process was an evolving trust in each other and in my organizing skills as the project lead, as well as our ability to identify and acknowledge what each participant brought to the process. Sharing personal and professional narratives, as well as stories and experiences related to things we care about and would like to change, were important elements in building trust with each other and in the process. Story and dialogue become the main ways in which project participants shared knowledge, skills, resources, and ideas, and cocreated project goals and action strategies.

Utilizing practices from narrative inquiry (described in detail later in this section), sharing stories functioned as ways of learning and knowing that were key to the development of new knowledge about questions we wanted to explore and actions we could take as a collective. I think of narrative inquiry as knowledge seeking and creation through personal and professional stories, in the context of each project. Scott Peters from Cornell University, Ana Elizabeth Rosas from University of California, Irvine, and Mekada Graham from CSUDH all use narrative inquiry in their work.[3] More directly related to community organizing, Marshall Ganz from Harvard University makes a strong argument about the powerful role that story plays in organizing for social change. Inspired by these and other writers, I too have been highlighting narratives and stories of people involved in my work for many years.[4]

Main Stakeholders

In line with the main stakeholders in civically engaged scholarship, participants in the five projects included faculty, students, administrators, and community partners. Some administrators and project funders, although not always fully involved as participants, played a significant role in supporting and allowing for the evolving of cocreating learning spaces that were the foundation of the projects. This is to say that in all projects, I, and often faculty, students, and community partners involved, received some kind of compensation in the form of stipends and/or course release. I strongly believe that this contributed to the deep commitment and engagement at least for two of the projects, which lasted two years. As stated in previous publications, my organizing focuses primarily on tenure-track faculty as the starting organizing point, because I believe that they have an immense untapped potential for developing collaborative civic agency to improve their institutions and the community at large. They also are more likely to stay in their institutions much longer than administrators and students, and they, through tenure, enjoy much more job protection than non–tenure-track faculty. I do acknowledge and celebrate that there is a growing movement to create more equity for non–tenure-track faculty, which may lead to their involvement in long-term, reciprocal civically engaged scholarship as well as more involvement in working for institutional change.[5]

Through my practice and research, I have discovered that faculty (including civically engaged faculty) are not always aware of their potential for building collective civic agency to create institutional change, for a number of reasons. One reason for this is that we have a predominant academic culture that rewards activities and deliverables and does not value collaboration and process, and we have bought into this paradigm. This culture exists outside of academia too. I strongly believe that in order to create culture change in and outside higher education, we must recognize that this has been socially constructed and can therefore be deconstructed. Although we may feel powerless, I argue that we are not victims of this circumstance. We have agency, and can use it especially through collective agency, difficult as making this paradigm shift may be. I also believe that faculty must learn to work with and recognize what other stakeholders can bring to the process of creating reciprocal partnerships. Equally important, students, administrators, and community partners must learn to engage in conversation with each other, and with faculty as cothinking, cocreating partners. There are, of course, isolated cases in which this multi-stakeholder cocreation process takes place, but this is not the norm.

Purpose and Methodology

The larger context of this book is my work of several decades as a community organizer in and outside of academia, and my work as a civically engaged scholar. In a way, this book is the sequel to my first book *Transformative Civic Engagement through Community Organizing*, where I shared a civic engagement approach that is based on community organizing practices I used at Occidental College, during my doctoral research at Maynooth University, and while completing my postdoctoral research at the University of Southern California.[6] In this second book, I expand by sharing how organizing combined with research methodologies underpinned the five projects shared in chapters 3 through 7, which were introduced in the previous chapter. They illustrate my ongoing organizing efforts to create collaborative spaces where collective leadership can emerge through research in action and narrative inquiry, combined with community organizing. These projects took place within a period of six years.

I mentioned in the previous chapter that I first realized community organizing practices had a strong resemblance to my current academic research methodologies during my doctoral studies. Prior to this, I saw my research simply as an organizing practice. So, when I started my doctoral program, I thought I had to learn research from scratch. Luckily, my academic advisors in the Department of Adult and Community Education at Maynooth University knew better. With their guidance, I began to see the similarities between community organizing and participatory action research (PAR, contextualized in the following section). What a discovery. What a gift! My doctoral research was in fact a combination of community organizing and PAR, and through this process I realized community organizing has relevance for academia, not just for communities outside of academia. I also realized then that research exists, and has always existed, outside of academia. The latter just is not always labeled research, nor is it common to refer to those using research methodologies outside of academia as researchers. This important discovery marked the beginning of my path as a civically engaged scholar. It gave me the language and methodologies to merge my organizing and research roles in an organic way.

PAR resonated with the process I described in the campaign story in the previous chapter, and narrative, in-depth interviews commonly used in PAR to collect data resonated with the one-on-one meetings through which I learned about issues that matter to the people I was organizing with. This also resonates with the story sharing that takes place in the one-on-one meetings, and with narrative inquiry. This discovery was life-changing for me, as I realized that PAR gave me language to "speak organizing" with faculty who may not be as comfortable with nonacademic terms and methodologies. This has been helpful especially at the beginning of my civically engaged scholarship. In most recent years, I have found a way to be open and direct with participants inside and outside academia about using community organizing language.

Research in Action and Narrative Inquiry

Research in action is a form of participatory action research (PAR). PAR is one of many terms used when referring to research that involves participants in the process of inquiry and has a social justice orientation. Other terms include action research, community-based research, emancipatory research, and community-based participatory research. To McIntyre, these "are all variants of PAR that traditionally focus on systemic investigations that lead to a reconfiguration of power structures, however those structures are organized in a particular community."[7] Writing about collective leadership from an indigenous perspective, Chellie Spiller, Maunganui Wolfgramm, Ella Henry, and Robert Pouwhare add that in the process of this type of participatory research, researchers and participants are also cocreating knowledge.[8] This process of cocreating knowledge fits with narrative inquiry "as a way of thinking about, and studying, experience" as stated by Clandinin and Huber.[9] The authors add that through the telling and retelling of stories between researchers and participants, creating change is possible at multiple levels, including social, cultural, institutional, and linguistic. This definition of narrative inquiry resonates with the process we experienced in my five research projects.

As I got to know my partners and coauthors in this book and listened to their personal and professional stories, I realized that many of them are using similar types of research methodologies to PAR and narrative inquiry. One example is Sarah Taylor, an associate professor of anthropology at CSUDH. She participated in the faculty learning community that focused on creating community-engaged syllabi and or class assignments that integrated arts, humanities, or design. Taylor's ethnographic research on community-based tourism development in a small town in the state of Yucatán in Mexico uses PAR and narrative inquiry. In her book *On Being Mayan and Getting By*, Taylor tells the stories of what residents of this small town experienced over a period of several years while their government tried to implement an economic development plan based on tourist attractions. In a small town where most residents are likely to know each other, Taylor decides to use ethnographic allegory to keep residents' confidentiality as much as possible. This is how she describes it: "Throughout the book, we will visit the Ay Mena family seven times. Each visit provides a glimpse of a day in the life of this family at a specific point in time in relationship to the process of tourism development in the village. This is a fictive, composite family made up of the real actions and words of actual people in the community. . . . This composite family of fictionalized individuals represents the real experiences of various residents." Through her ethnographic approach, Taylor artfully, skillfully, and powerfully transports readers to the daily routines of her research participants by providing a "rich, thick description of the lived daily experiences residents have with tourists and tourism."[10]

Writing as Inquiry

I mentioned in chapter 1 that as I began to work on this book, some questions arose about what took place in the five projects beyond my own interpretation, and that made me realize I would need to reflect on those questions with project participants. This led to the desire to explore collaborative writing as a process of inquiry, with the aim of continuing my organizing role in building collective leadership. I knew that I could do what I did while working on my first book, namely, interview participants from the five projects and write up excerpts from the interviews. This did not feel like collaborative writing.

While looking for models and definitions for this type of writing, I found resonance in a paper written by Ken Gale and Jonathan Wyatt titled "Working at the Wonder: Collaborative Writing as Method of Inquiry." In this paper, the authors distinguish between this type of writing and research and writing collaborations in which many academics tend to engage but that focus on the finished product and not on the collaborative process. This type of collaboration has an inherent ambivalence, the authors note, whereby academics are required to develop collaborations, on the one hand, "and on the other [are] inhibited in doing so due to neo-liberal academic institutional processes that privilege individual achievement, progression and promotion." Given this ambivalence, the authors write about collaborative writing "not as the commonly viewed task of 'writing up' research findings, but as a method of inquiry in its own right."[11] I decided to look for examples of this type of writing and found several books written in dialogical format, such as *Breaking Bread: Insurgent Black Intellectual Life* by bell hooks and Cornel West, and *We Make the Road by Walking: Conversations on Education and Social Change* by Miles Horton and Paulo Freire.[12]

Inspired by these and other writers, I invited project participants to reflect and write with me about their experiences in their respective projects. Several of them agreed to do this, and they are authoring the chapters describing the projects in which they participated. Some of them are also collaborating with me in the final manuscript of the book. Our collaborative writing draws on several group and individual phone and online conversations with my coauthors. These conversations centered on questions and themes that include our views, experiences, and thoughts regarding the extent to which we were able to create collective leadership and to what end; their views and experiences with and about research in action and narrative inquiry; the role of personal stories in our work; the roles they played in their specific projects; and whether the intense moment we were all experiencing in the summer of 2020 due to the pandemic and the anti-racist movement influenced our retrospective reflections about our work in the five projects, and about what is needed to create culture change in general.

Our conversations about the projects were recorded, transcribed, and edited by participants, based on my feedback to their iterative drafts. I followed up with further conversations with chapter authors as needed. In the methods we are using to write it, this book offers an invitation to explore an approach that seeks to use a collaborative, experiential way for us to learn how to work, think, strategize, and take action together, across disciplines and across sectors. It is offered to inspire and inform efforts to build collective leadership in order to create culture change in our institutions and communities. Circling back to my two questions at the beginning of this chapter, my hope is that the five projects will give readers a sense that they too can find ways to create their own spaces where they can collectively embark on efforts to change parts of the culture of isolation and fragmentation that plagues our institutions, organizations, and communities.

While the book focuses primarily on projects related to civically engaged scholarship,[13] the approach we used is transferable to academic initiatives not related to civic engagement, as well as to initiatives outside of academia. Our ability to tap into our civic agency, and to transform our individual agency into collective agency, is of paramount importance to the work of enhancing and mending our fragmented democratic society, and the ways it affects our personal and professional lives, our institutions, and our communities. Our book borrows from many civic engagement scholars, and it builds from my own practice and scholarship in civic engagement and community organizing. During the five research projects, and while writing the book, I have felt that the sense of community, respect, and trust that these combined practices and concepts can create are not just rigorous, intellectual, and practical collaborative work. They can also feel magical and spiritual. This is certainly how they feel to me. This work is food for my soul.

I now turn to the chapters about the five projects. I frame each chapter with a brief background of how I met the authors and what made me want to ask them to collaborate with me on this book. While writing these introductions to my colleagues I felt a great deal of warmth and closeness to them. I felt I could communicate this by using their first names.

Notes

1. In my institution's current work developing a strategic plan for the university, community partners were intentionally included as stakeholders in this process.

2. In these times of COVID-19–related remote work (2020–21), faculty have had to make rapid and radical adjustments to their teaching, and many are expressing that they are falling behind with their research and publications. This has also had a significant effect on civically engaged scholarship as faculty try to figure out how to engage their students with community organizations remotely.

3. See, for example, Scott J. Peters, *Democracy and Higher Education: Traditions and Stories of Civic Engagement* (East Lansing: Michigan State University Press, 2010); Ana Elizabeth Rosas, "Undocumented Emotional Intelligence: Learning from the Intellectual Investment of California's Undergraduates, *Boom California*, December 7, 2017, https://boomcalifornia.org/2017/12/07/undocumented-emotional-intelligence/; Mekada J. Graham, *Reflective Thinking in Social Work: Learning from Student Narratives* (New York: Routledge, 2017).

Marshall Ganz, "Public Narrative, Collective Action, and Power," in *Accountability through Public Opinion: From Inertia to Public Action*, ed. Sina Odugbemi and Taeku Lee (Washington, DC: World Bank, 2011), 273–89.

4. See, for example, Maria Avila, "Reflecting on and Sharing Our Stories Can Transform Society," in *Asset-Based Community Engagement in Higher Education*, ed. John Hamerlinck and Julie Plaut (Minneapolis: Minnesota Campus Compact, 2014), 17–30; Maria Avila, Adriana Aldana, and Michelle Zaragoza, "The Use of Counternarratives in a Social Work Course from a Critical Race Theory Perspective," in *Routledge Handbook of Counter-Narratives*, ed. Klarissa Lueg and Marianne Wolff Lundholt (London: Routledge, 2020), 255–66; Paulo Freire, *Pedagogy of the Oppressed* (New York: Continuum, 1995).

5. My institution, in a collaboration between the Academic Senate, the California Faculty Association (our union), and the administration, has made several changes to increase equity for non–tenure-track faculty within the past five years, including inclusion in the Academic Senate, compensation for participating in university committees, and developing a path toward tenure-track positions.

6. Maria Avila, *Transformative Civic Engagement through Community Organizing* (Sterling, VA: Stylus, 2017).

7. Alice McIntyre, *Participatory Action Research* (Thousand Oaks: SAGE, 2008).

8. Chellie Spiller, Rachel Maunganui Wolfgramm, Ella Henry, and Robert Pouwhare, "Paradigm Warriors: Advancing a Radical Ecosystems View of Collective Leadership from an Indigenous Māori Perspective," *Human Relations* 73, no. 4 (2019): 516–43.

9. Jean Clandinin and Janice Huber, "Narrative Inquiry," in *International Encyclopedia of Education*, 3rd ed., ed. Barry McGaw, Eva Baker, and P. Penelope L. Peterson (New York: Elsevier, in press), https://www.academia.edu/4559830/Clandinin_D_J_and_Huber_J_in_press_Narrative_inquiry_In_B_McGaw_E_Baker_and_P_Biographies (accessed February 14, 2022).

10. Sarah R. Taylor, *On Being Maya and Getting By: Heritage Politics and Community Development in Yucatán* (Boulder: University Press of Colorado, 2018), 13.

11. Ken Gale and Jonathan Wyatt, "Working at the Wonder: Collaborative Writing as Method of Inquiry," *Qualitative Inquiry* 23, no. 5 (2016): 355–64.

12. See, for example, bell hooks and Cornel West, *Breaking Bread: Insurgent Black Intellectual Life* (Boston: South End Press, 1991); Myles Horton and Paulo Freire, *We Make the Road by Walking: Conversations on Education and Social Change*, ed. Brenda Bell, John Gaventa, and John Peters (Philadelphia: Temple University Press, 1990).

13. To clarify, the project related to creating an organizing culture for the staff of a school board member describes how this took place, but the project was part of my civically engaged scholarship. Also, the project about integrating community engagement in the general education curriculum is coauthored by a community partner.

3
Discovering Collaborative Research in Action

Kathleen Tornow Chai and Enrique Ortega

Authors' Background

I met Kathy (as I have known her) and Enrique at a college retreat during my first year at CSUDH, and just before beginning a project with the Kettering Foundation focused on exploring ways in which civically engaged disciplines can/should contribute to enhancing democracy. I remember being struck by Kathy's passionate statements about the connection between nursing and social justice. I was curious to learn more about what she meant by this and followed up with her after the retreat. In our meeting, I shared more about my interest in exploring the ways in which she considered nursing to be a civically engaged discipline, and whether or not the discipline contributed to creating a more democratic society. During this conversation, it became clear to me that I wanted to invite her to my research project. I had an opportunity to talk with Enrique during one of the breaks we took at the retreat. He shared that he was on the faculty in the Community Health Science Department, and the community part of his discipline piqued my interest. I wanted to know what this meant for his teaching and research. He mentioned that he had worked with community organizations surrounding the university, studying ways in which his research could connect with health issues related to the work of these organizations. Enrique mentioned he would be interested in exploring an opportunity to pursue research grants together. I did not know what this meant, but this gave me the opportunity to follow up to continue our conversation. I discovered then that Enrique had a very humble way of describing what I considered civically engaged scholarship. He seemed to feel that his community engagement was transactional on his part, and that he had not really explored a more reciprocal or mutually beneficial way of partnering with community but he would like to learn how. This really struck me, and it made me want to bring this perspective to my research project.

—Maria Avila

The project we write about here opened our eyes to collaborative research methodologies; to the need to have more democratic, collaborative spaces on our campus; and to the value of our narratives as educators. At the end, this experience was, perhaps unexpectedly, transformative in many ways. In this chapter we will discuss *collaboration, the use of personal narratives, narrative reflection, and research in action.*

This project was a collaboration with the Kettering Foundation, and its focus was to explore the ways in which various disciplines engage with the larger community, and to underpin the process with community organizing practices. We met several times during the fall of 2015 and the spring of 2016. Our meetings included reading, reflecting, and discussing our views and thoughts about civic engagement, especially related to our disciplines, and specifically related to Kettering's research question, "What does it take to make democracy work as it should?"[1] There were eight faculty members from various disciplines, including nursing, community health sciences, occupational therapy, social work, human services, labor studies, and negotiation, peace, and conflict resolution. In an effort to include voices from various stakeholders related to civic engagement, there were also two social work students and one community partner. The authors of this chapter were participants in the project. Kathleen Chai was at the time chair of the Nursing Department. Enrique Ortega is associate professor in health science and, as of the writing of this chapter, associate dean of the College of Health, Human Services, and Nursing.

Given our disciplines, we shared a common understanding of a research methodology that is heavily based on the use of empirical and quantitative evidence. The training in our disciplines proved to be an initial point of friction with the methodology used in this project. Many of the following reflections denote the culture change and transformation we both underwent as a result of our exposure to the project's methodology and goals.

Why Are There Not More Collaborative Spaces?

Prior to 2015, cross-departmental collaboration was rare in the College of Health, Human Services, and Nursing, and other than annual faculty retreats or participation in college-level committees, there was little contact with fellow professors in the college. The college is made up of twelve units that are housed in multiple places around the university campus. While some departments are housed in joint areas, others are scattered throughout the university and even at a stand-alone industrial building fourteen miles from the university's main campus. Graduate and undergraduate programs are offered, and most are traditional face-to-face class offerings, some during the day and some in the evenings and on weekends. The Department of Nursing is an exception, with most classes being offered primarily online with a few hybrid courses that utilize the nursing skills lab. Faculty office space is at a premium, and while tenured and full-time faculty are usually provided an office, shared offices for part-time faculty are not uncommon. Below, we share our experiences as we began participating in this project.

> *Kathleen:* I remember being invited for a one-on-one meeting to follow up on a conversation we had about tenure and community organizing at a college faculty retreat. Our mentor, Maria Avila, communicated that the charge of the project was to develop a community organizing process to assess faculty interest in civic engagement; expose them to civic engagement concepts and practices, including Kettering research; identify civically engaged faculty; and begin building relationships with students and community partners. After our one-on-one meeting, I was looking forward to collaborating with her on this project. My initial understanding of the project was intriguing in that it seemed like it offered a way to integrate the voice of the community into setting the direction of academic research. As we began to meet as a group, project participants learned about each other's service learning and other types of community-engaged work, and we were amazed to learn there were several similar projects and even some that overlapped each other. One of my thoughts during this initial meeting was: Why are these types of meetings not happening on a regular basis? Learning what other programs were working on was invigorating and gave me a sense that there were great possibilities for research collaborations in front of us. For instance, occupational therapy students were working with a community organization, beginning to assess their health care and development needs, and students from the School of Nursing were looking for ways to provide community health services as part of their clinical involvement. Sharing was eye-opening and stimulated some of the team to think of ways interaction with other departments would be possible to benefit students.

As an experienced nurse, I was also relatively new to academia. Several years prior to this project, I had tried to initiate a cross-departmental project that would have two departments sharing qualitative and quantitative research classes. The other department had a strong research program, where nursing was rather weak. As junior faculty, I proposed this idea and was immediately told it would not work. The greatest concern was over the calculation of teaching units and financial benefit to the department. I learned then that collaboration and sharing were not a natural part of academia.

Enrique: My introduction to the project also began with a one-on-one conversation with Maria, which started with her asking about the nature of my current research and my role within the university. The introduction to the project included references to *community participatory research*, a term that was well known to me given that such research is commonly referenced in public health. Nonetheless, it was references to *civic engagement, democracy in action*, and *collaborative leadership* that led me to believe the project embodied a richer, more inclusive understanding of the term "community." By the end of our conversation, the seemingly simple question "What role does the community play in your research?" led me to consider that the answer to this question required much reflection about my present research practices.

The first group meetings were highly valuable to my sense of community within the college and the university. I had initial questions that were indicative of the experiences I felt would benefit me and my colleagues across the university: Why are there not more of these types of meetings? Why is this the first meeting of this type that I have attended? Learning about the ongoing work of other programs was invigorating and allowed me to consider a number of possible research collaborations. I considered that this was a definite marker of change for my view of the role that community and dialogue plays in the direction and practice of academic research. I remembered expressing that the opportunity to sit with colleagues and reflect on the manner in which we have included the community in our academic efforts was a rare privilege. It struck me and others as odd that such a valuable experience would not be a common practice of our academic lives. My initial understanding of the project was that it would offer a way to better integrate community voices into processes of academic research. While I had been in contact with local communities through various research endeavors, it was this project that began to reinforce the idea that many of these contacts were far from ideal and that this could change. Many of my collaborations with local communities tended to be framed in a constrained academic environment. Indeed, many of my experiences collaborating with communities had a swift transactional nature. Unfortunately, it had been my experience that many community stakeholders and community members viewed academic research and academic researchers somewhat suspiciously. It was not uncommon for community partners to relate to me their experiences of being "used" for research and soon forgotten after the completion of projects.

Fortunately, not all of my community collaborations have been transactional or fraught with mistrust. I have had the privilege to be a part of strong working relationships between academia and community partners that were characterized by respect and trust. These efforts have always been characterized by yearslong relationships that were built through side-by-side collaborations on many projects aimed at achieving shared objectives. The initial description of the project promised to show me a way to integrate community voices into academic research directions from the outset, as partners.

Academic Enculturation: Our Professional Narratives

Kathleen: My full-time entrance into academia came after teaching for over fifteen years as part-time faculty while finishing my doctorate and establishing my independent business of consulting in health care quality, a field in which I developed an expertise early in my career as a nurse. I consulted across the country and internationally, while also teaching for the national association that accredits hospitals. I worked both independently and collaboratively with other experts who consulted in the same field.

In 2009 I entered the university as a full-time faculty member. I applied for and was accepted as the undergraduate coordinator for a program that had over a thousand online students. These were all nursing students who had completed their initial nursing certifications but did not have a baccalaureate degree. My teaching load was half time with administration making up the other half. Obviously counseling a thousand-plus online students was more than a half-time job, but that is all that was allocated at the time. I moved most student contact from phone calls to online to facilitate communication, to be able to reach more students.

The process of continuing to teach presented some obstacles. However, since I was tenure track, I learned that there were many more responsibilities of a faculty member I did not know about. I jokingly referred to the tenure-track process as academic hazing. While I understood generally what scholarship and service were, no one really oriented me to what that meant. I did not receive a formal orientation but instead picked up things through emails and side conversations at the monthly eight-hour faculty meetings. The meetings were long, the atmosphere was somewhat negative, and I remember after sharing at one meeting and receiving negative feedback and even a profane comment, I felt it was better not to speak. My first file review and every one thereafter until I received tenure were uncomfortable and demeaning. I found myself having to rebut each one until tenure was achieved. What I did not understand until much later was that service, all the things I was doing to support the undergraduate students, meant little to the reviewers. They were much more interested in publications, even though the university was classified as a teaching institution, not a research university. Expectations were not clear, and therefore sharing and using a collaborative model were not valued.

Enrique: My work in academia has represented a stable environment that has offered me the opportunity to grow and mature both as a professional and as a person. At the time of this project, I was completing my tenure process, and my research and other professional activities were putting me in contact with a growing number of local community representatives. I have always valued collaboration with local communities. Community collaborations have served to put me in touch with the end users of the many theoretical or academic activities that consume my professional life. However, it seemed like many collaborations were set up so that each faculty member could get what they needed on their hurried paths toward professional promotion.

While the teaching loads of the university and the service and scholarship expectations offered me a good guideline to develop as a professional, I did not have a strong model on how to integrate such activities while balancing my attention to a growing family and wanting to build a purposeful career in public health. As many others did, I treated my professional activities as separate from my personal life; I would go so far as to say that I actively kept them separate in order to protect and foster each of these spaces independently. I believe that a driver of this type of thinking was a fear that my work would encroach and put demands on my family time and responsibilities. What I had not considered up to this point was that both of these sides of myself were connected to a singular story and that, as such, my story could be used to better understand choices and commitments to my work and my home life alike. Much more powerfully, through Maria's project I began to understand that my story could be used to thread together my work and home activities into a singular pathway that could help me build the purposeful career I was looking to establish. While this goal is an ongoing effort, I am consistently invigorated by examples of people who actively reflect on their family's histories and heritage in order to shed light on who they are and who they are becoming. Maria's project has allowed me to understand that sharing my narrative and intentionally practicing my profession with civic and democratic actions can help me bridge different aspects of my life into a common effort that is coherent and true to why I chose a profession in public health.

Research in Action and Community Engagement

During the spring of 2016, the second semester of the project, the group began to discuss research in action and participatory action research, and participants shared publications related to this methodology. We discuss here projects we shared.

Kathleen: I was able to share a publication by a nursing student who had presented a project based on her public health class. In the clinical portion, working as a nurse within the prison system, she recognized that inmates who were diabetic had little encouragement to control their disease. She developed a program to educate inmates and supply them with the necessary tools to manage their diabetes in prison.

This project helped me relate the community practice within nursing clinical experiences to the benefit to the wider community served. Prior to this, my opinion was that the students would benefit from these experiences by expanding their point of view to include actual situations and activities. By reflecting together in the group, I understood that the benefit also translated to the community and the impact the student ideas had on them.

Enrique: At that time of this project, I was conducting research in collaboration with a local Samoan community health agency in which we were exploring how that community's practices were associated with obesity patterns. This collaboration was typical of my previous partnerships. The greater research directions had been established in response to securing funding to respond to a documented health crisis in the community. Early research steps rarely included firsthand voices or reflections of community members. Rather, others pored over existing literature and reports to eventually strategize with community stakeholders on the best ways to elicit community experiences and practices that can shed light on the factors that are driving a health marker of interest. While public health science theory speaks much about the importance of forming bonds with communities and engaging community stakeholders to drive trusted and ethical research practices, my experience is that these practices are a challenge for many researchers in the field.

While I had sat on numerous focus groups listening to community members relate their lives to try to capture people's experiences with a particular health state, this was among the first times that I saw the potential of holding open conversations around the primary direction that my academic research should take. This, of course, would be complicated; personal research directions are often decided from personal passions and detailed discussions with colleagues, and in response to available funding trends. Nonetheless, in earlier conversations the question was asked why community voices should be excluded from these early stages in research—especially in research conducted at a public university whose funding comes from the state itself.

Narrative Reflection and How It Can Change over Time

During our online reflection session about this project, we were able to compare and contrast our roles in the university then and now, and lessons we have learned especially in the context of the COVID-19 pandemic and the Black Lives Matter movement.

> *Kathleen:* At the time of this project, I was the chair and director of my department. I felt that I was behind the rest of the group in understanding the purpose and engaging in a completely different research approach than I had seen before. However, now I have stepped out of that leadership role, and I am also

partially retired. One of the great things about retiring is that you have time to reflect and see what impacted you then that you did not recognize. Now, I do not have to be in charge. Back then, I felt the responsibility for the whole department, not with the project, but with everything else I was doing that I was responsible for, and we were heading toward the School of Nursing's accreditation. So it was a very pressure-filled time. Now, I can look back and see that over the last couple of years I realize that I have tried to build in ways for others to become involved and own the different projects. I think that is one of the positives about collaborative research and listening to other people's stories. When others affirm your perspective, it is validating.

Two very important things have happened since the project took place, and they have caused me to reflect even more deeply. The first was the COVID-19 pandemic. I see that it has changed the way the health care system works, the way people respond to everything from science-based information to what is deemed as political interference. I am still teaching and feel the pain the nurses experience with the deaths they frequently confront and the anger displayed when diagnoses and treatments are rejected. I have seen students in the College of Health, Human Services, and Nursing adapting to the new reality that will eventually transition the entire health care system.

The second major event was brought to a head with the George Floyd murder. The university is a Hispanic-serving institution, and the majority of faces on campus do not resemble mine. I did not realize in my first thirty years that I was brought up in a very narrow, white, conservative environment. I have to say, 2020 was the first time I said to myself, "Why have I let all these white men dictate what I'm thinking?"

I have certainly grown and changed over the years, even leaving one rigid Christian denomination for a more liberal one. I always saw myself as sensitive to diversity as I was married to a Korean gentleman and we raised our children together. The events of 2020 have caused me to reflect on why people I know do not seem to understand what is behind all the anger and frustration. My church recently hosted a six-week virtual book club called White Fragility, focused on Robin DiAngelo's book of the same name.[2] I am not sure that without these major events I would have been as interested in the topic. I know more why I teach than why I'm a nurse. I dropped out of nursing school six weeks before graduation the first time but found that I love teaching. In fact, I often share the narrative about starting nursing unsuccessfully with my students, as I think it helps them consider that success is not always easy. Teaching, to me, has always been something I could do to give back. I grew up with a family of preachers and teachers, so it kind of came naturally to me. I am a lot different. I've come to realize that unless you recognize, first of all, yourself and what your culture has led you to believe, it's very hard to see that somebody is different from you. One of the things we're talking about in this book club is white privilege. White people don't always understand that they have white privilege because they've never not had it. There is no such thing as Black privilege. Recognizing what you've been gifted with inherently or why things make you comfortable and uncomfortable, you also have to recognize how other people are feeling about some of the same things. I plan to incorporate experiences and questions related to these two major events into my classes in future years.

Enrique: As I reflect back to when this project was taking place, I realize that as an assistant professor in community health, I valued top-down directions and clear assignments of project goals and tasks as well as having timed benchmarks to show one's progress to completion. This structure was present in my advancement through tenure, in research projects, and in most activities conducted within the university. This format of benchmarks, goals, and specific aims has been embedded into nearly everything I have done in the field, from preparing manuscripts to seeking grants and showing satisfactory progress toward established goals. This was one of the reasons that I found this project incredibly valuable yet confusing at times. I valued the process that was being clarified as meetings progressed. However, the passing of group meetings without an apparent charted direction or ticking off objectives would often leave me confused and worried that the project was not progressing beyond the group having great conversations and reflections on community engagement and participatory research. At that time, I did not understand how conversations could translate into specific changes in my research practices. I pointedly recall an early project activity where each person was asked to "share their story." I recall asking why we were doing this and wanted clarification on how this activity was tied to a specific project goal. At this point, a graduate student that was more accustomed to these types of tasks explained how she valued expressing her life story in class so that her lived experiences could be valued and integrated into course activities and even as a part of the learning experiences for the group. Our mentor explained that her and other students' stories served to humanize their coursework and that these stories allowed them to make the coursework their own. Her elaborations made me reevaluate my view of storytelling and began to see the incredible value that such an activity could play in my research practices and with my research assistants. At that time, I had an average of five to seven undergraduate research assistants.

The task of a narrative reflection is powerful and requires the participant to be fully engaged in a way that conveys trust in the research process and in fellow participants. As I received the prompt to think about and share the stories and events that were formative to my evolvement as a professional and a researcher, I began to make a conscious decision to be fully present and open in my recollections and in sharing my story. I did this in hopes that this could allow me to understand how my story could contribute to a project's direction. I began to recognize how my personal narrative was woven into my evolvement in the university. My evolvement through the tenure process and my greater involvement in college and university operations has been intimately tied to my home life. My greater involvement in university life was mirrored by my evolvement as a father, husband, and son. My increased responsibilities at the university have paralleled the greater home responsibilities that came with the births of my two sons and with the evolvement of my marital life. My home life has required me to find ways to provide a space where one can nurture people through their own evolvement. I have noticed that I have begun to carry this perspective as a course instructor and with my research assistants. Reflecting on my narrative allowed me to understand what personal strengths I could bring to the institution and to my role as an academic and an administrator. The classroom is a place that requires consistent effort to make it inclusive of people's abilities and varying levels of engagement and understandings. The personal reflections that came from this project allowed me to consider that students come to the university holding experiences and qualities that are unique and varied in their relationship to high educational attainment. These unique contributions can lead to richer experiences of learning among groups of people who can empathize or learn from different life stories. My role as an educator and a research mentor began to move away from pushing a single achievement standard that was meant to help students align their output to what was needed for entry into graduate school or employment. Instead, I began to accept students' academic evolvement on an individual basis and encouraged them to reflect on what they wanted to achieve and how such goals were aligned with their lives and those of their loved ones.

Collaborative Leadership and the Future

We feel that this introduction to collaborative leadership has colored the way we see the current academic structure. We have both experienced the negative feedback from other faculty who, when approached, wonder what we are bothering them about or what we might be taking from them. It seems as if others often feel that in sharing, they will give something away that they might otherwise have received credit for. Instead, both of us have found that sharing with and bouncing ideas off each other has expanded our perspective and allowed us to have more ideas and information than less. Both of us have been given the opportunity to hire new faculty and have used this experience to choose those who seem willing to work in a collaborative way.

As we discussed this and what we could do to influence others to try a collaborative process, we recognized that sharing our experience, what we have learned, and how we have changed or planned to change our approach might interest others in attempting to move forward with a similar type of project. In the field of health care disciplines, there is a movement toward interdisciplinary education and collaboration, as described by the Institute of Medicine.[3] Many universities are slow to adopt this concept, and the tradition of siloed departments remains. Providing faculty within the college with our example may spur others to increase collaboration and reach across departments to combine resources for research. A proposal for this presentation is being developed at this time. We initially proposed a working session with representatives of all departments to the dean. In this session we would describe the process that we went through at the beginning of this journey, including the one-to-ones. Then we would invite them to conduct their own one-to-one with a representative from another department. In the end, we would help them tie together what they had learned about each other and then relate it to a potential research collaboration. Follow up sessions would be offered focusing on narrative inquiry, community engagement, culture change and other areas that we found facilitate collaborative work. These are our thoughts about working together, and each of us will share our final comments.

Enrique: In my current administrative role, I have yet to fully explore how my narrative inquiry could foster building collaborative leadership. In this role, I interact with peers and people that are in higher positions of leadership. While the role of collaborative leadership was clear in my faculty position when I was dealing with students and research partners, this has not been the case in his present interim position in administration. For one, the tempo and nature of activities in which I am now involved do not always lend themselves for much opportunity to work with colleagues in extended timelines as is natural in the instructor-student partnership and in the research collaboration setting. This is where I can use mentoring from more seasoned democracy-in-action likeminded individuals to help me bridge these gaps in the practice of building collaborative leadership that is reflective of community participatory actions.

Kathleen: Now that I am no longer chair but still involved in the department, I can see the subsequent chair fostering collaborative leadership. Recently, at a faculty meeting it came up that faculty were frustrated with inconsistent scoring on graduate students' final activities and felt the need to change the process and parameters. In previous years, I would have asked for an individual to lead the change, form a subgroup, and work together to effect the change. The current chair did not do that. He allowed multiple members of the faculty to weigh in on what they thought needed to be done. The meeting exceeded the allocated time frame, and while a great deal of sharing had been done, no decisions had been made. The chair finally asked the faculty what they wanted to do, and they decided to schedule an additional meeting within days. The second meeting took place and again, after an hour, no concrete decisions had been made. However, the chair hung in there with the group, and finally, within two hours, consensus on the changes was achieved and everyone approved. Later I realized that this discussion facilitated collaborative leadership, which would have been stifled had the chair used my previous method of sticking to the time frame and handing off the assignment to a subgroup. This way took much longer; however, the satisfaction of those involved was significantly more than if the other way had been taken.

Tying these examples together, I decided to use the last year serving as our nursing honor society chapter president as a pilot for collaborative leadership.[4] At the beginning of the year the plan is to hold one-to-one meetings with each of the board members to ascertain their goals and expectations for the upcoming year. Reconfirmation of priorities will follow. From there, a plan will be developed and board members will evaluate the progress frequently as I will attempt to model the process used in moving us toward solutions. This will not be without challenges, given the significant amount of time it takes to work through the one-to-ones, small groups, and validations.

Enrique: I believe that collaborative leadership and an inclusive culture should be a fundamental aspect of any organization, but especially an educational organization that highlights novel inquiry and the production of knowledge. I believe one's narrative can be best integrated into organizational objectives through leaders who are intentional and committed about seeking collaboration from their activity partners. To me, this type of leadership must be balanced with the nature of the person's position in the organization and the activities at hand. In my experience, it is university leaders who demonstrate consistent actions of inclusiveness and elicit consistent shared governance that tends to have high buy-in to institutional practices. It is these same leaders who tend to act as stewards for the university and for personnel in a way that is immediately recognized. This type of leadership, though, must be balanced with the nature of the person's position in the organization. I personally have experienced occasions where people want and need their leadership to provide unambiguous and timely direction. There are occasions where people are looking for a division of responsibilities where the leader's tasks include providing a direction that others could follow. I definitely see the value of collaborative leadership, but in some cases, others (and note that it's situational) may not have that understanding of leadership or may not want the responsibility of collaborative leadership. At this point, my plan is to spend more time with research partners, really listening to what the community has to say. My goal is that the principal investigator is a full partner with the community. Again, I recognize that this might take more time or even change previous goals, but the end product may be more acceptable to the community.

Kathleen: I have a bit of a different perspective. In hindsight, while I believe that collaborative leadership is a useful, powerful tool, I also realize that many of the decisions I made as chair did not display that value. On further reflection, I recognize a few things. Collaboration takes more time than it does to act individually. Often due to external barriers, one does not have the time it takes to confer with others and wait for thoughtful responses. Or others may bring up points that the leader does not feel are valuable, and rather than working through them, the leader chooses to step in and end the collaborative process. That may be due to lack of time or the fact that the leader does not want to spend the time it takes to get to consensus. While it may increase expediency, it totally shuts down the collaborative process, which brings to mind comments Enrique made about participants feeling they were "used" for research processes and then dropped.

Was this exercise useful? It was for both of us. We have had the opportunity to reflect more thoroughly on both past and current leadership opportunities. One of the side effects of the pandemic appears to be that people have slowed down. There are fewer places to go, people to see, and opportunities to socialize. Some of that has been very challenging, but after a year into the pandemic (at the time of this writing, in early 2021) and a forced change of pace, it made sense to focus on people's stories, trying to understand different perspectives rather than coming up with quick solutions.

Finding others who are willing to work this way might be difficult, but we learned how to start. Maybe, as the adage goes, it is good to have a destination, but the real joy is in the journey.

Notes

1. Kettering Foundation, "Core Insights," https://www.kettering.org/core-insights/core-insights (accessed February 22, 2022).
2. Robin J. DiAngelo, *White Fragility: Why It's So Hard for White People to Talk about Racism* (Boston: Beacon, 2018).
3. National Center for Biotechnology Information, "5 Building Organizational Supports for Change," in *Crossing the Quality Chasm: A New Health System for the 21st Century* (Washington, DC: National Academies Press, 2001), https://www.ncbi.nlm.nih.gov/books/NBK222276/ (accessed February 22, 2022).
4. Xi Theta is the CSUDH chapter of Sigma Theta Tau, an international nursing honor society.

4

Igniting a Culture of Relationships and Collective Power in an Elected Office

Aixle Aman Rivera and Ray López-Chang

Authors' Background

I first met Aixle when the board member she worked for, and with whom I had partnered through my work at Occidental, invited me to train his staff in community organizing practices. The board member had been in his role only a year. Aixle and I met the following week to discuss further details of the project and to agree on the terms of a contract. We met for a couple of hours, and as it turned out, we only talked about the project and the contract toward the very end of our meeting. The rest of the time we talked about ourselves and our work, comparing our community organizing concepts. I learned then that Aixle had been trained in IAF organizing practices, and almost without knowing, she was using some of these practices in her role as a leader with a national organization of public educators. I met Ray shortly after I met Aixle, at a workshop where I introduced the project to the rest of the staff, and where I introduced them to my approach to community organizing. In this workshop I shared my story and asked them to share theirs. I remember Ray's almost unfiltered honesty as he shared his struggles as a young leader with the Los Angeles Neighborhood Council in the area where he lived.[1] He shared other leadership experiences since then, but this seemed to be a formative experience in his journey as a civic leader. He was passionate and energetic, and he wanted to learn how to be an effective organizer. Ray had a deep commitment toward his community and was happy to be a field representative for it through this new job.

—*Maria Avila*

We believe that the art of organizing is the most powerful tool we are born with. It is built on human connection, grounded in vulnerability and trust, and fueled by love. This chapter will be our humble attempt at catalyzing you toward a journey of learning this art. We are of the belief that there is another instance in our lives where we have learned something almost as rewarding as organizing. By the age of two, most children are learning to carve space in this world using their five senses. They are developing depth perception, learning to differentiate textures, and serving as master sponges of knowledge.[2] They are actively growing a proficiency of themselves and their bodies to define how they want to interact with the world. Most of us are too young to remember these experiences, but it is our earliest taste of power and our first step into life. Our hope is to show you that community organizing can be your second step. It feels that way for us.

We sought to create a community organizing culture with the Los Angeles Unified School District (LAUSD) Board District 5 (BD 5) team between 2016 and 2019. We attempted to do so after extensive training, observations, and reflections by and with Maria Avila on fundamental community organizing practices that would ultimately transform the way our office approached our work and the relationships we built with our constituents. The overall purpose of this project was to teach our staff how to build civic leadership in BD 5, using the community organizing practices we will discuss later in the chapter.

At the time of this project, Aixle served as the chief of staff, and Ray served as one of two directors of community engagement. In this chapter we describe the transformation of our office culture and the outcomes we hope to have achieved with our constituents. First, we position ourselves by sharing our personal stories. These narratives directly informed how we received this community organizing training and thus how we approached the implementation of the organizing practices introduced to us. We also discuss the power of narrative inquiry and its influence on our organizing practice. This was our first preview of translating self-reflection into professional application. Next, we investigate the process of culture change in BD 5 communities, located in Southeast, Northeast, and South Los Angeles. This culture change encouraged our team to shift from transactional interactions to a relational approach and required that we reassess the nature of empowerment versus the activation of power. Finally, we describe the power of relationships and its transcendence across BD 5 communities. If we are successful, by the end of this chapter you will gain a renewed perspective of relationship building, learn the synergy between your personal narrative and that of others, and reacquaint yourself with a kind of learning you may have experienced when you were a toddler. This chapter is not meant to answer your curiosities; it is meant to strengthen them. It also does not serve as a comprehensive guide to different organizing models or practices, but as a taste of the power of personal stories and their ability to catalyze relationships.

Connecting Our Narratives to Our Organizing Practice

Aixle: I have always believed in the power of collaboration and the power of the collective. I have activated this power through the acts of service I performed throughout my Catholic education and servant leadership, and over the last several years I have seen this power more than ever throughout my professional career.

As the daughter of Filipinx immigrants, I grew up in a Catholic household and attended Catholic school from grades 3 to 12. This is how I learned the value of being in community and doing more for others, especially those who have less than I do. From high school to college, I became actively involved in Christian leadership groups that helped organize activities for other students. Together, we planned engaging masses to which our peers could feel more connected (e.g., utilizing props, modern dance, and popular music). Because of this community, I never felt alone, and I could tangibly see the impact we were having on others through the acts of service we performed.

The values of service, community, collaboration, and deep listening have stayed with me throughout my professional career but have manifested themselves and been reinforced in different ways. As a former teacher, my calling was to serve my students by listening to their stories, needs, and hopes for themselves and their families. I needed to listen but also take urgent action. This need for urgency was reinforced by the organizing work I did in LAUSD BD 5 with former elected board member Ref Rodriguez. In Los Angeles I was able to truly consider and see firsthand the power and possibility of collective people power, as compared to positional power, to transform communities, so students and families can thrive.

Ref first challenged our BD 5 team to consider how we talked about and approached our work and relationships with our constituents. We initially focused our community engagement strategy on wanting to empower our communities. However, Ref shared with our team that he preferred we not use the word "empower" because, by definition, the word implied that we were *giving* power to others when they, in fact, already had it. Through our community organizing training, we reframed our thinking and adapted a relational approach to our work with our families instead of a transactional one. One of our biggest learnings was that everything is grounded on relationships and that our charge was not to empower our constituents but to *activate* the power they already possessed. The families and community members in BD 5 were rich with knowledge and expertise of their own communities' needs and opportunities through their lived experiences. It was our job to help them see their experiences as valuable assets that can catalyze them to take action to improve the conditions around them. As a team, we knew that if we could activate their power, our constituents would no longer need to rely on the positional power of an elected office to transform their communities. They could do that themselves.

I am fortunate that my current work at Leadership for Educational Equity (LEE)[3] allows me to continue applying my organizing knowledge and experience to support a national network of members as they build or deepen their own organizing mindsets as civic leaders in policy, advocacy, elected, and organizing roles. At LEE we see the potential for amplified impact when elected leaders ground themselves in an organizing-first mindset and work directly with community organizers to advance their equity-focused agenda. Moreover, we believe in a *collective impact* framework by which a cross-section of civic leaders collaborate to solve a shared problem focused on equity to ultimately achieve sustainable and transformative change in communities. This framework of collaboration has the power to disrupt systemic barriers that are the root cause of many educational inequities. While my doctoral dissertation focused on the *direct* impacts that community schools and their partnerships have on a child, my work with LEE extends this research to the political, cultural, and structural systems that have more *indirect* yet powerful impacts on the child. From the school site to a political office, people possess the power to reimagine and collectively transform their communities and fight for the world as they would like it to be.

Community organizing started off as a set of principles and strategies I needed to learn as part of my professional journey. Little did I know my understanding of community organizing, especially as a lens through which I view the world and not simply as strategies and practices, would penetrate every aspect of my life and every interaction I have with others. My deep listening skills have been strengthened by my organizing work, my professional coaching responsibilities, and my personal mediation practice. I tune in to what others are saying, feeling, and seeking in any given moment. Their stories become part of me and help shape my belief systems. I remain grounded and called to this work because of the stories and hopes of my former students, the BD 5 families, equity-minded civic leaders in the LEE network, and my own daughter whose story is yet to be told.

Ray: At the start of my organizing career, I remember feeling eager to absorb important cues that would help me excel as an organizer. To some degree, I felt like a sponge, again. I was working at BD 5 in service of the communities that raised me in Northeast Los Angeles. Early on, my experience was always *in service of*. It was rooted in my desire to develop a voice for others as I grappled with developing my own. That journey influenced the way I operated in my education government role, which was to be a communicator of student, parent, and educator needs. As I knew it, my job was to listen to the requests of the community and translate them to our staff, superintendent's office, division heads, and other board district offices. But sometimes the families I was working with in the community did not trust me. I considered this might be due to the politically charged nature that education politics have generated over time. Or that maybe I was witnessing the residuals of an immigrant culture that errs on the side of distrusting government.

This is especially important because most of the families I worked with were immigrants from different countries in Latinoamérica. In some ways, I resonated with how they felt having been raised in Nicaraguan, Chinese, and Salvadorian households. In the 1970s my mother's family fled as refugees from Nicaragua because my Chinese grandfather was on a government hit list for generating income as a foreign-born businessman, married to my Nicaraguan-born grandmother. My Salvadorian grandmother, too, left El Salvador to pursue a brighter, bolder future. I took note of her excitement and optimism toward Nayib Bukele's 2019 election as El Salvador's youngest, most progressive president. Her emotional response to progressivism illuminates for me the pending need for governments to budge.

My family's history affirmed that our BD 5 communities' distrust was justifiable. So, to do my job adequately, I had to meet families where they were. This is when the community organizing training I received through this project became the most important catalyst in my organizing career. I quickly realized I was embarking on a complex feat, facing families with deep wounds mildly healed by insufficient trust. Through this project, I spent the first two years of my organizing training learning the synergy between professional responsibility and personal authenticity. Sometimes, when we are at work, we are taught to leave emotions at the door, but organizing taught me to bring them front and center. I mastered this skill over time, and soon it became the basis of all my interactions in my continued career.

My first strategy was to pay attention to other organizers in the field. I became attuned to the techniques of good organizing: masterful communication, attentive listening, and consistent affirmation. At first, these traits appeared to be the basics of expressing kindness, but in the organizing world, I was challenged to add a fourth trait: *agitation*. This groundbreaking skill has become my bread and butter. This chapter will discuss more on agitation later.

After four years at BD 5, I transitioned to a role at the United Way of Greater Los Angeles (UWGLA), where I was tasked with organizing and managing a coalition of education advocates operating as a vehicle for educational equity. The Communities for Los Angeles Student Success (CLASS) Coalition consisted of twelve organizations that held a deep commitment to advocating for vulnerable students, families, and educators. There was no question about our alignment on educational equity, especially during the COVID-19 pandemic.[4] But organizing families in BD 5 was very different from organizing seasoned, executive, and senior leaders of an organization. I experienced impostor syndrome and questioned my ability to organize because my professional training on the ground suddenly became decontextualized. The audience and self-interests of both professional experiences were vastly different, so at UWGLA, I needed to swiftly adapt my organizing skills to activate the expertise of CLASS Coalition leaders. My hope is that throughout this chapter, we can unearth the diverse applicability of the organizing mindset. I had this realization soon after doubting my ability to reignite CLASS toward excellence. I made the decision to approach organizational coalition building similar to the way we built coalitions of families in BD 5: one-on-one meetings, bridge building, flipping transactional interactions into relational ones, and narrative inquiry.

My experience with CLASS illustrated the power of an organizing mindset as versatile, intelligent, and evolving. By no means did I feel ready for the remainder of my organizing journey, but I felt prepared. Today, I have the humble privilege of re-engaging this energy in my current role at Great Public Schools Now, as we build collective action with dozens of cross-sector organizations who are passionate about educational recovery and uplifting the next generation of Los Angeles.[5] Except in this role, impostor syndrome took a backseat.

Reimagining the Culture of an Elected Office

After our first year in office, we had already become accustomed to serving our constituents however they needed us. In many ways, it could be seen that we had a *transactional* relationship between our office and our constituents. They asked for help and we provided it to them. We helped parents address their concerns with accommodations at schools, we worked with principals to make necessary upgrades to their campuses, we worked with librarians to get more books for their school libraries, and more. In return, we invited our constituents to events that we were sponsoring, asked them to take surveys, and invited them to speak on behalf of specific items at public board meetings. Each of us gained something. But these transactions were temporary and would be forgotten once we left office. While we didn't know it at the time, we needed and wanted more out of these relationships with our constituents.

Through the training we received in this project, we realized that we needed to rethink our transactional interactions with our communities and instead focus on being more *relational*, especially if we wanted to see the true power of building strong, trusting relationships with our community members. We learned several fundamental organizing practices—one-on-one relational meetings, house meetings, power, agitation, and critical reflection—which we will discuss more in the next section. As the chief of staff, Aixle's charge was to operationalize these learnings for the rest of the BD 5 team, especially since this approach was new for everyone. At first, although our feedback and opinions about what we were learning were integrated into the training, we felt that we were strictly learners who reflected on our work and practiced what we learned. As we practiced, our trainer often observed our work in the field to offer feedback, inform our workshops, and provide individual coaching. In the final section, we will share how we adapted our experience into a community engagement strategy that would live on past the elected term of our office.

The foundation of our organizing work was grounded in strong relationships with our community members and with each other in our office. We shared our stories with our trainer and with our other team members, and we reflected on our stories' connection to our work. We were also asked to critically examine what types of relationships we had with community members in BD 5, and whether we knew their self-interests. It was important to learn their self-interests and vision for community transformation because it would equip our staff with the language and motivating force to activate their power. In the next section, we will discuss how we utilized the organizing practices we learned to understand our community members more deeply.

Strengthening Our Organizing Culture

Our community organizing training in BD 5 began with intensive workshops, where we studied fundamental organizing practices. This investigation of practices helped us reimagine the direction of our office culture. We did not know what we did not know, so our board member, Ref Rodriguez, who had worked on previous projects with Maria Avila (our trainer and lead of this project), brought her in to support our professional development. In the following section, we describe specific organizing practices that transformed our office and community engagement culture from a transactional to a relational approach.[6]

One-on-Ones, Self-Interests, and House Meetings

To build an organizing and relational culture as an office, we first needed to get to know our community members on a deeper level. We accomplished this through individual, relational meetings, also known as *one-on-ones*. As we mentioned, the overall goal of the community organizing training and utilization of the practices we learned was to identify community members who would become part of a civic leadership team with which our office would work closely. Most of this relationship building would occur primarily through one-on-one meetings. As a team, our one-on-one meetings were mostly informal conversations but with strategic and calculated goals of uncovering each individual's self-interests and determining whether they could become part of a collective of leaders to create transformative change. We experienced a surge of excitement finding leaders in BD 5 and identifying the various roles they would hold in this collective organizing work. Not all of our one-on-ones would surface community members who would play leadership roles, but they would serve an important role either way.

Having effective one-on-one conversations was more difficult than our team anticipated. We learned that it was more than just learning their stories—it was about understanding their *self-interests*. As we learned, a person's self-interests are represented by how they spend their time, energy, money; who they connect with and can call on at any given moment; what institutions they are part of; and what they value. We needed to ask deeper questions and operate strategically with our time while still facilitating authentic conversations with our community members. The goal of the relational one-on-one meeting was to learn what each person really cared about and why.

Each BD 5 team member was tasked with scheduling one-on-ones with community members we felt had a "following" and could turn out other individuals. We strategically selected folks whom others would listen to because we knew the time would come when advocating for community transformation would only be effective if they organized a large number of stakeholders to apply pressure on decision-makers. Knowing these shared wins required such methodology, one-on-ones became a high-pressure relay to build that collective power.

Early on, these meetings felt emotionally charged and difficult to navigate. We often found ourselves struggling to reclaim our time during meetings because we did not want to compromise our authenticity. At times, it felt inconsiderate to interrupt a conversation when a parent was sharing an intimate or vulnerable, personal anecdote. But, after several months, we learned that it was important to be responsible and respectful of others' time, in addition to our own. Time management incentivizes efficiency, action, and movement—three characteristics key to working for an elected office. But, most importantly, it builds trust.

After having multiple relational meetings with community members, our next step was to convene a *house meeting* where we could either bring several of them together, or where one of them could invite others that would listen to her/him. The goal of the house meeting was to have various community members surface issues they cared deeply about, so that we could collectively identify shared interests. Our BD 5 team held many relational meetings and a couple of house meetings over the course of the first year after receiving our community organizing training. At one house meeting, a mother of children in Southeast LA schools invited a couple of engaged parents to her home; one mother brought along her friend. While they did not know each other, they all felt strongly about sharing ways they felt their children's schools could be improved. At another house meeting, a group of parents in Northeast LA, whose children attended different schools, discussed ways they could become more coordinated with information sharing, especially if it was going to benefit their children's academic success. The house meetings were opportunities for our community members to hear directly from each other and uncover areas of alignment and shared interests.

Over time, we were grateful our team cultivated relationships and learned our constituents' self-interests more deeply through one-on-ones and house meetings. Ultimately, our goal was to build a larger following of leaders who wanted to improve and transform their school communities. We knew this would only be possible with the collective power of the people living in their communities. Our most important job was to activate their inherent power and bring them together to share their interests with each other.

Power. Understanding the intricacies of *power* is an extremely important organizing practice that we carefully unpacked as an elected office. We examined *positional power* (also known as "power over") and *collective power* (also known as "power with"). As a team that worked for an elected official, we possessed *positional power*. The perception of this positional power was often more than reality. Our constituents expected that we could fix their problems or at least ask the district superintendent to fix them. This perception certainly fed into the transactional nature of our office culture and our relationship with them. We knew that wielding and leveraging power was more complicated, and that our community members, as a collective, had greater power than our elected office. *Collective power* is the power of the people, of the masses. In organizing, collective power is stronger than individual power. This type of power comes from building collective leadership.

Agitation. We also learned how to strategically *agitate* others, especially during one-on-ones. As was true for Ray, this organizing practice became our office's bread and butter. We learned that agitation serves as a tool to deepen conversation, strengthen a relationship, and responsibly probe for more insight into an individual's core motivating drivers. Aixle realized that agitation can be a tool to inspire someone to share more deeply and explore intimate feelings or thoughts they may have not previously felt comfortable sharing in a one-on-one. During our training, we learned that agitation is meant to challenge complacency, so that we can get to a place of hope, inspiration, and energy, to work as a collective and create the world as we'd like it to be.

Organizers can use agitation strategically to incentivize collective work, but it is essential that this tool also not be abused or manipulated. Ray also believes that agitation can be inspiring. He sees it as inextricably connected to his narrative. For Ray, to successfully agitate is to transition from the emotional obstacles of conversational discomfort toward a place of conversational trust. It mirrors the growing pains of life, where we challenge ourselves to be vulnerable and raw, so that we can boomerang into action and growth. Of course, this takes an exuberant amount of critical reflection, but agitation is the genesis of becoming better at being our authentic selves. To us, agitation and critical reflection are at the bedrock of expert organizing.

Critical Reflection. Critical reflection is important to organizing work because its goal is continuous improvement. Organizing is fluid, especially since it is based on relationship building, so it is important that organizers consistently engage in deep, critical reflection to improve their practice and ensure they are assessing situations and their learnings objectively in their pursuits to meet communities where they are. We learned that critical reflection is the opportunity to digest our thoughts and ideas, especially as we are experiencing them in the moment, or shortly thereafter. It is essential in four areas: evaluation, accountability, power checking, and self-interest checking.

Critical reflection was especially important after our one-on-ones with our constituents. While we were advised not to take notes during relational meetings so we could be fully present, we were encouraged to take notes immediately following the one-on-one when we were alone, whether that may be in the car or as soon as we got to our next destination. The BD 5 team used these notes and reflections to learn more about our community members, to reflect on how our organizing practice was developing, to draw connections with what we heard during other one-on-one meetings, and to determine how these learnings aligned with our office's overall vision for the board district. We believe this process is something we need to engage with regularly if we are to grow professionally, personally, and as organizers. Critical reflection requires time and energy, but true community organizing will only be as effective as our commitment to reflection.

To this day and in our current work, we continue to elevate the importance of reflecting alone and in community with others by either doing formal debriefs with our colleagues or by engaging in individual writing in our journals. We are confident that this community organizing practice has and will continue to be one we will utilize in our personal and professional lives moving forward.

Operationalizing and Integrating Organizing Practices to Capacitate Communities

Our organizing work as a BD 5 team evolved tremendously over time. As we mentioned, we started with relational one-on-ones and house meetings, but we soon evolved this organizing work into what we called Family Problem Solving Groups (FPSGs) and Parent Action Workshops (PAWs). An FPSG (meeting several times over two or more months) was our organizing strategy where community members could engage in a proven process that would lead to tangible, action-oriented work. A PAW (three hours each) was our opportunity to concisely share with our community members the organizing practices we learned through our training. This section will further describe these organizing frameworks.

Family Problem Solving Groups (FPSGs). After many one-on-ones with our constituents, our team was eager to engage them in a process where they could make actionable changes in their communities. We sought alternative ways to ensure that we were leveraging our organizing skills more directly. One of our team members, Gabriella Barbosa, introduced a framework she previously used with the Center for Public Research and Leadership while studying law at Columbia University.[7] We adapted this framework to meet the needs of the parents in BD 5 school communities, which resulted in the FPSGs. Through the FPSG process, participants identified a problem they wanted to improve in their school communities, performed a root cause analysis of that problem, and brainstormed solutions they would implement to solve it. The process required about six to eight sessions for each cohort. Over the course of almost two years, we engaged five cohorts across several different communities in BD 5, including Northeast Los Angeles, South Los Angeles, and the Southeast Cities in Los Angeles County. The cohorts represented a wide range of interests and constituencies, including Latinx, African American, and Native American families and community members. We specifically recruited participants who were not overly active in their school (e.g., parent-teacher association president or a parent group chair) but who showed strong interest in wanting to improve their school communities. This was important to us because we believe there is catalytic potential in untapped hearts and minds.

The problems selected by participants in the five FPSG cohorts included chronic absenteeism of elementary-aged students, thin partnerships between schools and local businesses/community organizations, inadequate support for English learners, low parent engagement among African American families, and lack of sufficient resources for Native American students. The culminating project for each cohort was the development of an action plan that showcased a solution to their problem. Ultimately, they presented their action plans to school district leadership, including the LAUSD superintendent. We witnessed the individual leadership of each of our participants evolve over the course of our sessions. Their confidence in themselves and each other grew, and by the culmination of their cohort experience, they felt ready to tackle the problems they had identified. While this FPSG process was very impactful for both the participants and our team, we also felt constrained by the length of time and extensive resources needed for each of these cohorts.

Parent Action Workshops (PAWs). Given the limitations of the FPSGs, our team pivoted from the FPSG work to PAWs in our final few months in office. Our instinct told us we needed to spread our organizing knowledge across BD 5 as comprehensively, nimbly, and effectively as possible. We made the decision to shift from the FPSG framework to a tangible and concise model focused on building organizing skills. PAWs were constructed in a format that allowed our staff to offer three-hour sessions where we provided a high-level overview of organizing practices parents could use in their schools. We worked very closely with school administrators to ensure they knew we were not organizing parents against them. Rather, it was an opportunity to build the capacity of the parents to become better stewards of information and more adept at the intricacies of school issues. We would often dial up relationship-building components of the workshop and dial down the more technical skills of organizing. We felt that if there was only one message we could leave behind, it was that public, action-oriented relationships matter.

Both the FPSG and PAW work was counterculture for an elected office. We were no longer engaging in transactional practices and had become entirely focused on enabling our communities to do more for themselves. Our goal all along was to activate the power of our community members and equip them with organizing skills so that they would no longer need us to act for them. We hope we did just that.

Relationships as the Foundation: Trust Is Critical

Earlier, we mentioned the role that self-interests play in one-on-one meetings. However, we would like to take a moment to emphasize the importance of understanding self-interests to help us earn one another's trust. Self-interests are often driven by our own personal values, childhoods, and overall life experiences, including those of our families. During any given social interaction, we tend to assess one another's self-interests to determine the viability and direction of that relationship. In many ways, our self-interests dictate every aspect of how we present ourselves to the world. This is an important consideration because effective organizing requires conversations that push past the surface, which, although difficult, is only possible when we prioritize a communication style anchored in vulnerability.

We are highlighting vulnerability because it is the precursor to trust. By inviting our community members to share more about what they care about and what experiences drive them to take action, we were asking them to be vulnerable and trust us with this information. This is how we learned where their self-interests resided and why our relationships flourished. We quickly realized that mastering vulnerability was an essential element of mastering organizing.[8] During many one-on-one meetings, we found ourselves sharing our personal, perhaps traumatic, life experiences to create a brave space for others to offer their humanity too. This is powerful because when we allow our personal and professional lives to interact in this way, we create a new format for the relationship-building and trust-strengthening process.

These revelations affirm that our most important job as organizers is to responsibly access the voices of our constituents and enable them to realize their own power. We are reminded of the Southeast Los Angeles mother who shed tears during our one-on-one as she relived a traumatic sexual assault experience with us. We didn't take this lightly. We nurtured that relationship with deep care as she engaged in our organizing workshops. Today, we celebrate her staunch advocacy for her three children in both her personal and professional capacities.

We nourish relationships, engage vulnerability, restore trust, lead by example, and show what we've done so that others can organize for themselves. As we hope we have made clear, this is why no one has power to *give* to another human being. Expert organizers know this and are not in the business of empowering others. Our moral responsibility is to *activate* existing power.

Our Hope

Throughout this chapter, we described how trust and relationship building are critical to establishing an organizing culture among our elected office team members and the communities we served. Seeing BD 5 community members as thought provokers and community experts allowed them to trust us. More importantly, we learned to trust ourselves, first, to succeed at transformative organizing. Impostor syndrome plagued us both as we advanced through our careers, but we learned how to redirect this energy by grounding ourselves in our stories and history so that we could be reminded of our value and purpose.

We recall that as an LAUSD board district, constituents assumed we would simply resolve their problems. Initially, we believed this too. But our goal as a BD 5 team was to shift this expectation and construct a culture that was anchored in relationships. Our hope was also to build deep connections with our constituents by learning their self-interests through one-on-ones and house meetings and leveraging these self-interests to achieve shared goals. We remain adamant that this was only possible because of our unique and intentional journey of building trust together.

We are confident that our relational culture in BD 5 was built and deeply felt through our execution of Family Problem Solving Groups and Parent Action Workshops. Warren and Mapp describe how community organizing is an approach to addressing educational inequities by building power for underserved communities and tackling social issues inside and outside of the school walls.[9] We believe our relational community engagement strategy embodied this inside-outside power and collaboration to improve BD 5 communities. Through these FPSGs and PAWs, we saw firsthand our community members' power being activated. The fuel was already there; our BD 5 team lit the match.

By focusing our work on specific educational issues or on predetermined school communities, we were able to activate the power of several small groups of individuals committed to improving their communities. We now realize with the culmination of this chapter that although we worked to transform the lives of our BD 5 constituents, *they* transformed *us*, in immeasurable ways. We grew with them. We shared our knowledge. They soared. While our time in the BD 5 office has come to an end, we are confident our families will continue to advocate for their communities and fight for a world that allows children to meet their fullest and greatest potential. This is what gives us hope. And today, despite the stressors of this pandemic, hope remains our permanent agitator for educational equity and justice.

Notes

1. The neighborhood councils advocate for their communities with the Los Angeles City Council. They are part of the Department of Neighborhood Empowerment. For more information, see https://empowerla.org/councils/ (accessed May 11, 2022).

2. "The Five Senses," First 5 Los Angeles, February 11, 2021, https://www.first5la.org/article/the-five-senses/.

3. Leadership for Educational Equity (LEE) is a nonprofit leadership development organization inspiring and supporting a network of civic leaders to eradicate the injustice of educational inequity. More information can be found at https://www.educationalequity.org (accessed May 11, 2022).

4. Jen Wheeler, "CLASS Coalition Demands a Voice to Ensure Equity for Vulnerable Students and Families," United Way LA, June 23, 2020, https://www.unitedwayla.org/en/news-resources/blog/class-coalition-demands-voice-ensure-equity-vulnerable-students-and-families/.

5. "Educational Recovery Now: LA's Children and Schools Need a Comprehensive Plan," Great Public Schools Now, May 28, 2021, https://greatpublicschoolsnow.org/educationalrecoverynow/.

6. To read more about these specific practices and others, see Maria Avila, *Transformative Civic Engagement through Community Organizing* (Sterling, VA: Stylus, 2018).

7. The Center for Public Research and Leadership (CPRL) at Columbia University conducts high-impact consulting projects for clients in the education sector and provides rigorous coursework, skills training, and real-world experiential learning for graduate students who attend programs at Columbia University and across the country. More information can be found at https://cprl.law.columbia.edu/ (accessed May 11, 2022).

8. We learned the importance of vulnerability, but also that vulnerability needs to be calculated or strategic based on context. For instance, sharing an experience about sexual assault in a first relational meeting, for instance, may lead to discomfort that could cause the person not to be willing to meet again.

9. Mark R. Warren and Karen L. Mapp, *A Match on Dry Grass: Community Organizing as a Catalyst for School Reform* (New York: Oxford University Press, 2011), 5.

5

Regional Organizing for Culture Change

Alan P. Knoerr, Celestina Castillo, George J. Sánchez, and Rissi Zimmermann

Authors' Background

Alan was part of the faculty committee working closely with me during my tenure as director of the Center for Community Based Learning at Occidental College. At the time, he was an associate professor in the Mathematics Department. I had many meaningful interactions with Alan, but what struck me the most was his willingness to dig into his story, and his humble openness to learn from and with others. He was, and still is, very passionate about the role that mathematics can play to address issues of inequity. For instance, he was ready to do something about a problem we learned of in a regional organizing group I created in the area surrounding Occidental College. In this group, we learned that the high school dropout rate was alarmingly high and that there was a strong correlation between this and passing Algebra 1 by the ninth grade. In response, Alan led the efforts to create a course for Occidental College through which his students would work with students at area schools to assist them with mathematics.

I met Celestina in the early 2000s, as a student in a community organizing class I was teaching at Los Angeles Trade-Tech College, and she later became a community partner during my work at Occidental. She then became assistant director for the Center for Community Based Learning and became its director after I left Occidental. In this long-term relationship, we have learned about each other's stories, and through this, we learned to be supportive and responsive to things that most matter to us. Learning about her mixed Mexican American and Native American roots and about her multigenerational roots in her neighborhood has made a significant impact on my organizing interests and practices.

I met Rissi when I first created the Imagining America Southern California cluster. At the time, she was still a student at the University of Southern California, working closely with George Sánchez as her mentor. I first got to know more about her story while driving to a meeting from Los Angeles to the University of California, Santa Barbara (UCSB). I thought she could have a leadership role at the meeting at UCSB, but I needed to learn more about her story first. Rissi shared that she is originally from Germany and had learned to cultivate inner peace from her mother, who had Native American roots. Since then, I have continued to learn from Rissi about her commitment to work for inner and world peace through her art. She has shown an incredible thirst to learn and develop as a leader, from and with others in the cluster.

I met George at a civic engagement conference at the University of California, Irvine, where he gave the keynote speech. This was one of many times I heard him offer a civic engagement perspective that differed a great deal from more mainstream perspectives. George is still one of the few scholars that articulates so clearly and passionately civic engagement as it relates to marginalized, minority, and first-generation students. He helps us realize that many of these students have been civically engaged throughout their lives by virtue of living in disenfranchised communities, and that civically engaged scholars need to respond to them differently than we would to more privileged students whose college civic engagement experience may be their first exposure to working in marginalized neighborhoods.

—*Maria Avila*

Imagining America (IA) is a national consortium of scholars, artists, designers, humanists, and organizers whose stated mission involves imagining, studying, and enacting "a more just and liberatory 'America'" through public scholarship, cultural organizing, and campus change.[1] It was founded in 1999 as a collaboration of the White House Millennium Council, the University of Michigan, and the Woodrow Wilson National Fellowship Foundation to promote the values of reciprocity and mutual benefit in the growing higher-education field of community engagement, and to particularly encourage the participation of the humanities, the arts, and design. Currently based at the University of California, Davis, it has over seventy institutional members, including community colleges, small liberal arts colleges, and public and private universities across the country. Members benefit from IA research initiatives, virtual communities, publication opportunities, both undergraduate and graduate fellowships, an annual "National Gathering," and more local and regional events.

The IA Southern California Regional Cluster was organized by Maria Avila in 2015. While providing a space for regional members of IA, and others at local institutions contemplating joining IA, to build community, learn collectively, and think strategically about culture change, it also had practical objectives for the greater Imagining America national consortium. As the first regional cluster in IA, it has served to build networks between the various institutions of higher education in the region that could sustain conversations and dialogue between the annual conferences of the national IA consortium. These networks have allowed the cluster to create and strengthen additional collaborations between the campuses, which range from private universities to large public campuses to small liberal arts colleges to local community colleges. Part of the objective of the cluster has been to bring new campuses on board as IA members by adding to the value of membership through regional discussions on topics fruitful or unique to Southern California, such as the role of undocumented students or Latino-majority student populations, and by enhancing the experiences of campuses with IA. Founded with five members representing five institutions, by 2020 cluster meetings typically had more than ten institutions represented by students, faculty, administrators, and community partners.

The values of community, critical reflection, personal narrative, and collective leadership guide us in considering ways to shift the individualistic and competitive culture of academia toward one that inspires collective imagination, knowledge making, and civic action. The deliberately slow and intentional way we work together breaks with the usual demands in academia for high-paced productivity and allows us all to reflectively build the relationships and community needed to provide an enduring foundation for culture change.

In this chapter we first discuss benefits that institutions gain from membership in IA and the Southern California Cluster through the lens of our own experiences. Then we examine in some detail the organizing practices our cluster uses—focusing particularly on one-on-ones, narrative, collective leadership, group meetings, agitation, actions, and reflection—and the resulting additional benefits that individuals gain after becoming involved in our collective leadership. We illustrate this discussion using personal narratives and reflections of the authors of this chapter, all of whom have engaged with the cluster in this deeper way. Finally, we discuss some possible future directions for the cluster.

Benefits of IA and Cluster Membership

Campuses benefit from Imagining America and the Southern California Cluster in many ways. For universities with graduate programs, the Publicly Active Graduate Education (PAGE) Fellows program gives PhD and master's students the opportunity to join a supportive national network of graduate students interested in civic engagement.[2] The PAGE Fellows conference takes place at IA's annual National Gathering, and the network is further sustained through virtual meetings throughout the year. A wide range of interdisciplinary scholars participate in the PAGE program, which gives them training in advanced civic engagement while they are completing their disciplinary education at their respective campuses. Many of these PAGE Fellows from Southern California participate actively in the cluster as fellows, and some continue their involvement after their fellowship year. Indeed, some have gone on to become national IA leaders in civic engagement. Other campuses focus on undergraduate participation and our cluster's regular presentations and discussions. Undergraduates can take advantage of IA's Joy of Giving Something Fellowship,[3] and the Southern California Cluster has been instrumental in shaping more sustained and productive participation of undergraduate students at the IA National Gatherings. Beyond these institutional benefits, individuals involved in the cluster can benefit greatly from the networking and mentoring opportunities it affords.

Building Community through Sharing Stories

Understanding our own stories and engaging in dialogue about them grounds us in why we do this work and builds community by building respect for one another. Three of us—Celestina Castillo, George Sánchez, and Rissi Zimmerman—have been with the cluster from the beginning. In preparation for writing this chapter, we three had a conversation about our experiences as core leaders. What is it about the concept of culture change and this way of working together that we find compelling? We found that the cluster resonates with us because our life experiences have taught us to deeply value community. Communities have supported our safety, growth, and development throughout our childhoods, educations, and professional lives. We illustrate this here with excerpts from that conversation.

> *Rissi:* My passion for building community was framed by my immigrant mother who raised my four sisters and me to prioritize considering others' needs while exhibiting unconditional care for all life around us equally. Furthermore, growing up in a small town in Germany taught me how significant interconnected and long-term relationships are in creating community-centered infrastructures. Later my perspective on community expanded when I moved out of my home and to New York at age fifteen, building an international community that became my family. I learned how sensitive the process of bridging cultures is and how powerful relationships rooted in shared values that defy demographics can be. After being recruited as a Posse scholar at the University of Southern California (USC),[4] the lack of community within and beyond the campus unsettled me. My yearning to shift the power that fueled the separation I experienced between the institution and its surrounding neighborhood informed my educational path and future work.
>
> *Celestina*: The work I have chosen has been really informed by my mother and being in different spaces with her. The first six years

of my life were very connected to college with my mother because she had me when she was seventeen, and then went to community college followed by California State University, Northridge. While she was in college, it was all about culture, social change, and social movements. The purpose of everything was social change, pride in culture, and making changes in the world for our communities. The students went to school to learn about how to make changes in the community. Everything they did in work, in education, and socially was about making positive change for their communities. When I went through my own education, that is what I was looking for as well.

George: Coming back to Southern California twenty-three years ago I had to confront what it would mean in my life, where I was professionally and personally, to come back to where I grew up. I had already been committed to a research project in Boyle Heights, and what I really decided at that point was that I wanted there to be fewer borders between my work and my community. I wanted to find projects that allowed me to move between my research, my teaching, my mentorship, my service, my community work, all together because I was going to have this opportunity that most people, most faculty never have—to return to where they grew up. It put me in touch with a lot of things about growing up here, about who I was in the first seventeen years of life, now that I was mid-career. I had tenure, I had already produced a number of students, many of them from Los Angeles. What did I want the next part of my career to be? So getting involved in Imagining America was one part of that. I realized I had to learn from the right people; I had to be in communion with folks who thought in those terms.

The fourth contributor to this chapter, Alan Knoerr, joined the cluster in 2020 and was added to the core leadership team after Celestina and George had rotated out of this role. While Alan was not part of this conversation, community has also been central to his life.

Alan: My understanding of community has come from being between as well as part of different communities. I grew up in Durham, North Carolina, but my parents were from different immigrant communities in Milwaukee, Wisconsin (my mother's family was Greek, my father's grandparents were German). My father was a professor at Duke University, but my mother's mother had never had an opportunity for schooling in any language. I attended Durham City Public Schools under Jim Crow segregation. As that system slowly began to integrate, my family moved across town from the semirural working-class neighborhood of my childhood to the more affluent Duke Forest. I bussed to Hillside High School, the traditionally Black high school of the system. Rare among Black high schools in the South during this period of integration, Hillside remained largely Black and under the control of the Black community. As I later learned, Durham's Black community had a deep history of multifaceted relational organizing, which had enabled it to build an unusual degree of economic, political, and educational power from which I and my classmates benefited greatly.[5] My thinking in terms of systems and my relational work for social justice are rooted in these experiences.

Our common interest in community is not simply a search for a sense of belonging, networking, or friendship. We want to find others who share the same sense of responsibility to communities both inside and outside of the academy. We are interested in bridging these two spaces by creating knowledge and social change in both. Sharing personal stories helps us focus on these goals by gaining a better understanding of why they matter to us. It also helps us find authentic ways of doing this work.

Connecting Local Communities and Academic Institutions

The desire to connect the academy with local communities is another common theme for all of us and, of course, aligns with

IA's mission. Celestina and George are both from the geographic areas and communities where their academic institutions are located; this work has pushed and enabled them to connect with those communities in a different way. While their work within academic institutions has always been intertwined with the communities they grew up in, they have needed to navigate the cultural norms of the academy, which typically separate these two spaces. Neither Rissi nor Alan is originally from Los Angeles. On coming to USC as a student, Rissi found the separation between the campus and community very unhealthy. She believes the academy should share resources with our communities, as family. It did not make sense to her that the university and her peers would not feel connected to and responsible for the community in which the campus is located. In 1991 Alan joined the Occidental College Mathematics Department, which was at that time deeply engaged in grant-supported equity-centered curricular reform in partnership with some other educational institutions in greater Los Angeles. But it wasn't until 2005, when he began to get involved with Occidental's Center for Community Based Learning then directed by Maria Avila, that he began to connect with the local community and social justice issues in K–12 mathematics education.

We all gravitated toward academic institutions for different reasons but shared a hope that we would also be able to find a sense of community and a sense of collective responsibility for social change. George's commitment to social and cultural change is anchored in access, diversity, and equity. For Celestina, it is about acquiring the tools, information, and skills needed to address historic social justice issues in her communities. For Rissi, it is about encouraging human relationships to be heart-centered and always utilizing the arts to facilitate those connections. The domain of Alan's work is mathematics education, but his concern is with the power of truth telling and authentic relationships to transcend forces that create injustice.

The starting points and direct aspects of culture change each of us is interested in may vary, but we agree that it will take a collective effort to change our institutions and communities for the better.

Cluster Structure Emerging from Organizing Practices

The cluster helps us think and learn together about what culture change looks like and how to work in ways that will move our institutions. We are building a relational culture and power to change institutions by using organizing principles and practices to create and maintain the cluster. The organizing work of the cluster is a long-term project, with ongoing reflection and actions together that allow us to practice what we are learning and imagining.

The cluster is grounded first and foremost in long-term relationship building through one-on-one conversations and group reflections. Maria began building the cluster by meeting one-on-one with individuals from various Southern California campuses, choosing those she thought might be interested in a regional cluster aligned with IA's mission. After sharing personal and professional reflections through these one-on-one meetings, she invited representatives of five campuses to the first meeting in the fall of 2015. About a year later, Celestina, Rissi, Maria, George, and others gathered over a meal to reflect and share stories about the work of the cluster up to that point. "At this meeting, we agreed that those present would become the core leadership for the cluster, which meant collectively planning, strategizing, and facilitating cluster meetings." As Rissi remembers, "this was a space in which we could approach each other as human beings with equally valid intentions, aspirations, and emotions, and this is a space we continue to maintain in our meetings. This is not only an example of building community through storytelling but is also a step towards the public scholarship that IA promotes."

Our practice is that cluster members take turns hosting the meetings every other month. The host institution will generally make a small presentation focused on specific initiatives in which their students, faculty, and staff are engaged, and new people from their campus community often join the meeting. Other agenda items typically include one-on-one and group conversations on personal and professional topics related to culture change, community, and current events. In pre-pandemic times, a typical cluster meeting also involved sharing food and lasted ninety minutes. During the pandemic the bimonthly ninety-minute meetings continued virtually.

While the host institution has a role in planning the agenda of a meeting it hosts, it is joined in this planning by other members who are more deeply engaged in the cluster; we refer to them as our core leadership. This collective leadership practice is a significant element of our approach to organizing for culture change. Participation in core leadership is based on interest, alignment with cluster values, and the ability to commit the extra time this requires. (In addition to advance planning, meeting organizers typically debrief for an additional half hour after the meeting, reflecting on how it went and what we can learn from it to strengthen the cluster.)

This interest and commitment, however, are cultivated by our relationship- and community-building practices. By way of illustrating this, Alan first worked with Maria as a faculty member and chair of the Community Based Learning and Research faculty committee at Occidental College when she directed the Center for

Community Based Learning (CCBL) there. Celestina was initially a community partner of the CCBL, and then she was hired by Maria as the center's assistant director. When Maria left Occidental, Celestina became the CCBL's director. About a year later, Maria did a postdoctoral fellowship with George at his Center for Diversity and Democracy at USC. For her part, Rissi had been mentored by George as a Posse undergraduate scholar and was then hired to work with him when he was vice dean in USC's Office of Diversity and Strategic Initiatives. While relationships like these are between several generations of scholars and initially formed within academic hierarchies, our intentional relationship- and community-building practices, including our collective leadership model and a deliberate "less is more" approach to planning and conducting meetings, actively level these hierarchies and replace them with a culture of peers in our commitment to civic engagement and collaboration.

Since 2019 we have also had a lead organizer as a paid position funded by an annual stipend from the national IA office. First Celestina and then Rissi have served in this role. Lead organizers coordinate meeting logistics, maintain communication between cluster members, recruit new members for IA, and strategize with the national IA community. The national IA office recognizes a reciprocal value in advancing IA's mission and encouraging institutional members of our cluster to also become dues-paying members of the national IA organization.

Another important organizing practice is planning, carrying out, and reflecting on *actions* together. In organizing, an action is a collectively planned, time-limited, and intentional effort designed to achieve a certain goal. Our actions so far have all been in relation to the national IA organization. We have participated in several of IA's annual National Gatherings: our members joined a panel on broad-based and cultural organizing in 2016, facilitated a workshop about the development of the cluster in 2017, collaboratively presented civic engagement projects from seven member institutions in 2018, and, in 2019, organized a panel of students from three cluster member institutions who shared their community engagement projects. During the COVID-19 pandemic in 2020 the cluster hosted a webinar for IA members, titled *Creating Culture Change through Regional Cluster Organizing*. We are currently beginning to consider hosting the IA National Gathering in 2024. While all these actions involve disseminating information and bringing wider attention within IA to our work, the common organizing goal has been to strengthen our collective and to deepen its knowledge of organizing. These shared actions give substance to our shared devotion to meaningful community engagement and to our interest in learning from each other's diverse experiences. Talking freely with each other about challenges faced enables us to develop a shared narrative about both our achievements and disappointments along the way as the cluster has evolved.

Imagining and Practicing Culture Change

There is a range of understanding among our members of what culture change is and what it could look like within their institutions. Some members already have a good understanding of organizing for culture change when they join the cluster. Others begin to think about it through their participation in the cluster, particularly if they engage in it more deeply by participating in our collective leadership. For the most part, however, we recognize that this is our shared purpose.

We also share an understanding that the cluster is a unique kind of supportive space that functions in a very counternormative way. For some, the cluster is an opportunity to connect with others who approach the work of community-engaged teaching and scholarship in a way not easily found elsewhere. For others, it is a space for learning and practicing organizing principles. For all of us it is a community in which we can imagine the campus and world we would like to live and work in. Discussing and experiencing all these things within the cluster makes it easier to bring them back to on-campus teams that are working to create culture change within our respective institutions. One way of creating culture change is by living it. The more we can each live the culture we hope to see through our interactions within and beyond the cluster, the more the culture we imagine will come to exist. We share here specific examples of how this has played out for each of us to illustrate this point.

> *George:* I was struggling to find an effective approach to community organizing at USC for my own civic engagement work. I wanted to learn about methods and processes with a group that shared this commitment. This is what I found in the cluster—an opportunity to learn from others with different perspectives on moving across the boundaries of institutions and other communities. Observing collective leadership in action and then applying that practice to my own work has been an important part of this. The lack of hierarchy in the cluster has been striking for those familiar with the normal practices of institutions of higher education. At USC I was a tenured full professor and had already served as chair of my department and vice dean for the college, but this was an opportunity to learn from coequals in civic engagement. The way the cluster creates time to reflect and share stories has also been key to my continued involvement with the cluster. I often work so quickly that I ordinarily have no time to do this in other spaces of my professional life. My experiences in the cluster with collective leadership, reflection, and telling stories have led me to approach running meetings, holding discussions, and listening to others in new and more effective ways.

Rissi: My participation in the cluster has been an extended meditation on the meaning of *community*. I have come to understand community as people united by elements such as shared experiences, beliefs, dependencies, or geographic location. Identifying the elements of life that we share between an institution and the surrounding neighborhood allows us to understand how we are one united community. Community-based learning, from my perspective, is learning together with others with whom we are united. As we meditate on the life we share with the broader human community, every experience and interaction we share with another person is an opportunity for community-based learning, be it at home, or in a public space, an academic institution, or a prison. *Culture* is an ever-evolving expression of values shared by a community, conveyed through the interactions forming the life of the community. Therefore, *culture change,* to me, means a shift in these common values.

I hope for a spiritual shift, a shift to a greater awareness of the spirit that is the unification of our creation, not just with other people but with all living and nonliving things, all bound together at each moment by matter and energy. Through this awareness, I believe, we can learn to improve our collective well-being, which naturally can improve our individual well-being as a result. For me, the primary value of education is to increase our awareness of the state in which life is passed forward through our own conscience, actions, and words, and through this process to develop an understanding of how to care for the well-being of our interconnected life force.

I have been grateful to be a part of the cluster because I have found it to be receptive to my focus on these values and have experienced it to be an expression of them in many ways. Our shared perspective on education as a process of learning how to improve the well-being of our communities is what keeps me participating in the cluster. The focus of our collaborative work is always on *each other* rather than the individual.

Celestina: As I have navigated my own education, I have always sought out others who believed that education was for community and not just for oneself, for the generations to come and to maintain the contributions of generations that have passed. When working at Occidental's Center for Community Based Learning (CCBL) I was excited to be in a place that used an organizing model and framework for community-based learning and research. The model and approach allowed for an ongoing process of finding and working with others who believed higher education is about building relationships, shifting power, telling untold stories, and creating social change, and it is rooted in collective responsibilities. The cluster has a similar culture and purpose.

This is not a typical approach to organizing; it is based on building relationships to build collective power and agency but does not always define specific issues or campaigns it is trying to win. It can often be difficult for others to recognize that it is not solely policy change that is a win but also long-term reciprocal relationships that create opportunities for collective thinking about how to change the culture of academia. Shifts in relationships and understanding of collective responsibility for social change are equally important and positive in the long run. I see addressing issues of individualism as the biggest change we are making. My hope is that students and colleagues will come to think about process and purpose differently, and to focus more on building long-term reciprocal relationships rather than short-term transactional ones.

I have witnessed such shifts in the students I worked with in the CCBL. After working with some of them for several years, I could tell that they had taken in concepts of organizing for culture change by the way they pushed back on conventional ways faculty and administration engaged with the community, and by always advocating for collective and reciprocal relationships with off-campus communities. For example, in 2019 student leaders and organizers for diversity and equity on campus pointed to the CCBL as a model for reciprocal relationships and partnership with communities and as a foundation for academic experiences for BIPOC students at the college.[6]

Alan: I met Maria at Occidental College in the early days of the CCBL. At that time I was a tenured associate professor of mathematics. More than a decade into grant-supported equity-centered curricular reform in that department, I was frustrated by the gradual loss of the progress that had been made as senior leadership in the department retired, the grants ran out, and administrative turnover at the college shifted institutional priorities. Maria invited me to a meeting of the Northeast Los Angeles Education Strategy Group (ESG), which she had founded to bring together educational leaders in the communities surrounding the college. I was deeply impressed with the way these meetings were facilitated, using processes already discussed in this chapter, and I tried this out in an interdepartmental faculty committee on quantitative reasoning I was cochairing at the time. The approach was so successful, both in strengthening relationships between committee members and in what that committee was able to accomplish, that I knew I had to learn more. In the ensuing years I continued as a member of the ESG, frequently chaired the Faculty Committee on Community-Based Learning and Research that supported the work of the CCBL, and codeveloped a community-based course called Math, Education, and Access to Power that I taught for many years. Through that course we partnered with One-LA, the local affiliate of the Industrial Areas Foundation (IAF), as well as with both the Algebra Project and the Young People's Project, two national organizations dedicated to pursuing social justice through math education.[7] What I learned through working with the CCBL and the ESG transformed my teaching and opened the world of community-based work to me.

This was complemented by the IAF community-organizing training that I undertook along with Celestina and other ESG members. This deeper study of community organizing, together with an emphasis on reflection and reciprocal relationships, enabled the CCBL to not only survive once Maria left Occidental but also to have its work recognized as a "high-impact practice" that is forming the core of the proposed new Center for Engagement with Los Angeles at the college. Through all this involvement, I have come to recognize and value this work as a way of knowing that is both akin to and as profound as the scientific method. One-on-ones, relationship building, and collective leadership help us identify deeply held common interests and commit ourselves to pursuing them together. *Agitation*—provoking emotional and conceptual insight through probing questions or challenging information—shifts prior beliefs and helps us form hypotheses about possibilities for change. *Power analysis*—the systematic analysis of power relevant to an organizational goal for the purpose of developing effective tactics to achieve that goal—enables us to effectively plan actions to test those hypotheses; these are our experiments. Debriefing and critical reflection following an action are our data analysis.

I am now emeritus at Occidental, but I continue to do some part-time teaching there. My new involvement with the cluster is an opportunity for me to reengage with these fundamental ideas and use them to strengthen my current organizing work with the Algebra Project in Southern California and with non–tenure-track faculty at Occidental.

Changing Institutional Cultures

While this chapter has focused so far on developing a culture within our cluster that reflects changes we would like to see in our institutions and society more broadly, we have also had some success changing culture at each of our institutions. The cluster, and the information and practices we learn through our involvement in it, have made us more effective at organizing with others.

George: I've applied the process of collaborative leadership to my ongoing work at the Boyle Heights Museum (BHM),[8] which

I cofounded in 2016 in the East Los Angeles community of Boyle Heights with community partner Josefina Lopez, founder of the community-based theater CASA 0101. The BHM is designed to develop historical exhibitions that can tell the history of Boyle Heights in the community itself. For each exhibition, a collaborative team of faculty, staff, community members, undergraduates, and PhD graduate students does research, visits archives, writes exhibition scripts, curates a new exhibition, and eventually mounts a full exhibition in the lobby of the community theater. Each exhibition also has an online component and produces public programming to draw audiences to the exhibition to discuss the issues raised by the history displayed. The BHM has evolved into a leadership collaborative in which students, staff, and faculty all share in running weekly meetings, engaging equally in organizing research and writing for the exhibition, and brainstorming programming events as a critical part of each exhibition.

By the fall of 2020 the BHM had produced three historical exhibitions using this collaborative approach to leadership and was working on its fourth exhibition focused on entrepreneurship in the local Boyle Heights community. I regard this as the best collaboration I have developed, working with students and other participants who are involved because they are getting something out of it for their professional and personal lives. The ways that BHM addresses community and academic concerns flow from what I have learned through the cluster. This has been a new experience for me—letting go and letting others take things in different directions—because as a faculty member I'm used to being in charge and responsible for coming up with everything. Being part of a collective working on a project means creating a space in which others can achieve what they want to achieve. This is not something I learned as a faculty member but rather through watching other people work, particularly in the cluster and in Imagining America.

Shortly after Occidental's CCBL was founded in 2001, its staff and associated faculty recognized that a change in the faculty handbook would be needed to institutionalize the culture change we hoped to achieve. Community-based learning and research needed to be explicitly recognized in this way in the faculty tenure and promotion process. But a change to the faculty handbook like this could only happen once significant culture change had occurred. Only then could it garner the faculty votes needed for its adoption. The CCBL, and the faculty committee supporting its work that Alan frequently chaired, had had these handbook changes as a long-term goal for more than a decade before the time seemed right to go for it. In 2013 an opportunity to make changes to the faculty handbook arose because it was time for the college to apply to the Carnegie Foundation for reclassification as a community-engaged campus.

> *Celestina:* I and the faculty committee used a process informed by community organizing practices to achieve this change in handbook language. The effort was led by faculty who had already invested in community-based learning and research, and we used this initiative as an opportunity for them to deepen their ownership and leadership of the work on campus. Over the course of a year, we met with various faculty in small groups to discuss the proposed language, identify any potential concerns, and make edits to address them. Meetings were convened with faculty governance, the academic dean, and other faculty involved in community-based learning and research to discuss and further refine the language. The most important conversations were with faculty who had reservations about community-based learning and research. Face-to-face meetings with these faculty provided an opportunity to address any concerns they had about what the language would mean for them and their work. Most of these conversations resulted in further edits incorporating their suggestions. When the time came in May 2016 for the general

faculty to vote on the proposed handbook revisions, support was unanimous. This slow, deliberate, and robust process of conversation and relationship building rested on years of work with faculty and administrations to change the way the college engaged with community and to greatly broaden the extent of this engagement. It contrasted strongly with the way that issues are normally brought before the faculty for a vote, and that in itself represented significant culture change. While the work of shifting the culture at Occidental is ongoing, this vote to change the faculty handbook language marked a pivotal moment.

I became involved in the cluster during this process. Initially the cluster was especially valuable to me as an opportunity to network and to think with people at other local institutions about the work of community-based learning and research. My involvement in the cluster helped me, on reflection, to understand this change in faculty handbook language as culture change rather than as simply a change of policy. But culture change is an ongoing process. I realize a lot of work is still required to shift perceptions and increase the understanding across campus of community-based research, in particular, so that these language changes will translate into substantive changes in how faculty are evaluated for tenure and promotion.

When Rissi experienced the doubtful spiritual connection between members of the USC community, she was led in 2013 to cocreate a safe and supportive space where other undergraduate students craving the opportunity to express what they were experiencing internally could come together.

> *Rissi:* At the first meeting, a group of about twelve of us met at a student's home. Sitting and lying on the ground in a circle that evening, each person shared why they felt called to join the gathering, what lived in their hearts that needed to be expressed and processed. Shortly after the conversation began, genuine emotions were flowing. We embraced each other, listening attentively to the

sharing of vulnerable stories. An hour passed or maybe two . . . the shedding of tears and laughter gave time no significance. After everyone had shared the now-unified energy of the circle naturally transitioned into a creative flow. We began stretching, dancing, drawing, and playing music. The exchanged emotions fueled the cocreation and sparked ideas for collaboration. As we found ourselves back in a closing circle, we summarized common themes that connected our experiences and spoke about how we could practically share these reflections through our creations with our larger community as an audience. Next steps naturally emerged as each person was eager to move forward in creating the visions that came to them. From then on, the space continued to unfold and grow into a collective known as Sokamba.[9]

Initially my peers at USC and I (representing various fields and schools such as the arts, sciences, social sciences, humanities, political studies, engineering, etc.) would meet regularly in circles to share reflections and cocreate performing art shows, ranging from twenty to forty creating participants per project. These shows took the form of interactive programming, events, and workshops. Our collective organically grew beyond USC as students involved started to graduate and continued collaborating on creating experiences with folks and organizations throughout the city spanning various ages and identities. Through organic relationship building and conversation, Sokamba secured fiscal sponsorship as a nonprofit organization from the Center for Conscious Creativity and was recognized as an official USC partner through the university's Joint Educational Project (JEP). In this partnership I was able to codevelop (with students, colleagues, professors, teachers, and staff) a Sokamba program through which USC students facilitate weekly workshops at the local Vermont Avenue Elementary School, guiding second graders in creatively reflecting on their values and in expressing their emotions and visions for their families and communities.

Current projects are focused on building outdoor educational and healing spaces, co-led by local community organizations.

Experiential workshops and creative programs take place in various neighborhoods throughout the city, partnering with schools, universities, family-owned businesses, nonprofit organizations, and for-profit organizations. This includes partners, students, and members who otherwise could identify as homeless, famous, rich, undocumented, Democratic, Republican, doctor, formerly incarcerated, and so on—the point is that in Sokamba we are all seen simply as sisters and brothers, all interacting with, through, and for the cultivation of love. Everyone who is called to the community contributes what they can in return for what they receive. Sometimes this is monetary but more often it is time, love, food, shelter, "citizen-ship," skill, knowledge, land or other resources, and care. In these exchanges, we embrace the recognition that we cannot *exactly* measure the dimensions of our experience (such as numerically defining time, space, or energy) and trust that if we give out of love we will receive within love. The community is a living and breathing interwoven web of relationships that is ever-evolving in its definition while being rooted in the values of equal reciprocity. In my understanding and experience, the cluster is an extension of this interwoven web, cultivating balanced exchange of life experiences rooted in mutual care. I especially value the cluster for the continued love, recognition, and encouragement I receive from my mentors within the cluster by supporting the path I have chosen for my continuing education.

Alan: I joined the cluster virtually during the COVID-19 pandemic and while I was teaching online for the first time. I found that the techniques I had learned through the CCBL and ESG for building community and strengthening relationships adapted well to online teaching. They enabled me to develop a supportive culture in these classes and effective relationships with each of my students despite the challenges of interacting only virtually during stressful times. On financial grounds, Occidental made the unfortunate decision to furlough many staff during the pandemic. I helped organize an online faculty-staff alliance that created space for staff to voice their feelings about what was happening, and which considerably strengthened individual faculty financial support for an emergency fund the college had set up for furloughed workers. Because of my organizing experience and nontenured status as an emeritus professor, I was also elected to the Non-Tenure-Track Faculty Committee, which is working to give voice to that much-abused and recently unionized segment of the faculty. But my primary current organizing work is with the "We the People" National Alliance / Math Literacy for All,[10] created in recent years by the Algebra Project to bring together organizations across the nation dedicated to advancing social justice through math education. Our local chapter currently includes teachers, professors of mathematics, professors of math education, and other education leaders representing a broad and deep range of experience in this area. There are core relationships at the heart of this group that have developed over many years, and we are using some of the techniques of the IA Southern California Cluster to advance this issue-focused work. I have thus found that the organizing principles practiced by the cluster can be adapted to a wide variety of settings.

Evolution of the Cluster

We will focus now on two aspects of the evolution of the cluster, one rooted in process and the other in circumstance. We've talked about our collective leadership model, but now we want to highlight the active mentoring this fosters. Hierarchies tend to magnify the faults of those at the top and stifle the contributions of those at the bottom. With horizontal collective leadership we are free to teach and learn from each other according to our abilities and our needs. This keeps the cluster vital by helping us move forward individually, which in turn makes it possible to move forward collectively in response to internal initiatives or changing circumstances. Everyone involved in cluster leadership has seen their roles change over time. After her fellowship finished at USC, Maria became a tenure-track faculty member at CSUDH. As her responsibilities there increased, Celestina took on the active convener role for the cluster. When Celestina left Occidental and started graduate school at the University of California, Los Angeles, Rissi took over the cluster leadership while also leaving USC to become the artistic director of the Sokamba Performing Arts Company. As Rissi's commitments with Sokamba and other teaching opportunities have increased, Alan has assumed a greater leadership role. This change is part of a natural progression, and that's a very positive thing.

The challenges of the COVID-19 pandemic and the antiracism movement triggered by the murder of George Floyd and other African Americans at the hands of police, not to mention the escalating problems of climate change and other issues, have highlighted the need for culture change and created opportunities for it. We need to dig deeply into what democratic process means in this context, beginning with a recognition that the American public includes communities that might not speak English. Southern California can offer a lot here in learning how to engage with and reach this underappreciated part of the public. These conversations need to start at a neighborhood level, and institutions of higher education need to relate to their neighborhoods and communities in new and different ways. We must also recognize that a substantial portion of the American public is more interested in hanging on to its privileges than in democracy. States are banning teaching about racism—this is fundamentally anti-democratic.

IA's long concern with these issues and our cluster's grounding in repurposing organizing principles for higher education position us well to respond to these challenges. The relationships we had established in our cluster prior to the COVID-19 pandemic enabled us to continue and grow when we were forced to meet virtually. The process-intensive approach we use is a good way to think about how to emerge from the pandemic. The way we talk with each other, develop relationships, and foster a culture of mutual respect is a good way to think about change and how to do things differently. That is our focus—how to change our institutions rather than how to "help the community." It's about starting with yourself, then changing your relationship to your institution, then changing the relationship of your institution to the people it works with outside the academy. This applies equally to those engaged, as some of us are, in creating alternatives to the traditional academy. The questions are: What is the world as it is? What would you like it to be? And part of the answer is the culture change you can make, not just by participating and showing up but through public scholarship broadly construed.

Our organizing practices and the relationships we've built with each other using them position us well to respond as a cluster to these broader changes and challenges in society. But we still need to do this work. The mission of Imagining America is broad, and as a result people come to the cluster for many different reasons. As we emerge from the pandemic and can look forward to renewing our practice of meeting in person, we recognize a need to define more explicitly our own mission as a cluster and to align our leadership practices with that mission.

Culture Change Takes Time

Culture change is a slow and intentional process. It results from a long-term investment by a collective of people dedicated to thinking, imagining, practicing, and reflecting together over a period of years.

There are short-term wins that can emerge from the collective, but they are not the overarching goal of the work. Short-term wins and projects are motivating and important, but they do not in themselves signal that the work of institutional culture change is done.

An example is changing the tenure and promotion language in Occidental's faculty handbook to include community-based learning and research. When such a change was initially broached with the dean of the college in 2001 in the early days of the CCBL, we were told this could never happen. The criteria by which faculty are evaluated for tenure and promotion are central to defining the institution and had never been changed in living memory. Nonetheless, because the faculty had the power to vote for such a change, we recognized it would be possible if we organized to change faculty culture. Over more than a decade, through four presidents and many more deans, the CCBL and the Faculty Committee for Community-Based Learning and Research built faculty support directly through workshops and faculty learning communities, by supporting faculty across many disciplines in their community-engaged teaching and research, by building strong reciprocal relationships with community partners to provide opportunities for this work, and by partnering with faculty to secure outside grants. We also built support indirectly by building student demand through very positive experiences with community-based courses and undergraduate research opportunities, and by having the quality of these experiences documented through both internal and external assessments.[11] By the time of our final campaign for the handbook language changes in 2013, community-based work was recognized throughout the college as a highly successful "best practice" and was prominently featured in our marketing.

The handbook language changes were thus both a win for that final effort and an indication that a certain degree of culture change had occurred among Occidental faculty over these many years. But on another level, it was only an indication of a potential for broader culture change in academia. Ongoing, long-term work is still required to create a culture that values knowledge created in the community as much as that created in the academy, and for community-based research to be valued equally across academic disciplines.

In this chapter we have endeavored to give the reader some insight into the culture-changing work of our Southern California Chapter of Imagining America. We have shared our personal and collective goals, the practices at the heart of our community, and the individual narratives of four cluster leaders: how we came to this work, how we've experienced it within the cluster, and how participating in the cluster has strengthened our work with our home institutions. We've also shared some thoughts about the next steps of our evolving work and organization.

One thing we hope the reader will recognize is the interplay between unity and diversity. We are unified in our recognition of each other's humanity and in our commitment to practices that we've found help us experience and effect culture change. But our experiences in coming to this work and how we participate in it are quite diverse. We see this diversity as a measure of the value of the principles that guide us.

Notes

For an earlier account of the Imagining America Southern California Cluster, see Celestina Castillo, "Building a Regional Cluster for Cultural Change in Higher Education: The Imagining America SoCal Cluster," September 2020, https://iagathering.org/mainsite/wp-content/uploads/IA-SoCal-Cluster-Regional-Organizing-Paper.pdf.

1. Information in this paragraph about the national Imagining America organization, including selected direct quotes from its mission statement, was taken

from its website, Imagining America: Artists + Scholars in Public Life, https// Imaginingamerica.org (accessed July 9, 2021).

2. Imagining America, "Publicly Active Graduate Education (PAGE) Fellowship," https://imaginingamerica.org/what-we-do/fellowships/page/ (accessed July 9, 2021).

3. Imagining America, "Joy of Giving Something (JGS) Fellowship," https://imaginingamerica.org/what-we-do/fellowships/jgs-fellows/ (accessed July 9, 2021).

4. The Posse Foundation, "About Posse," https://www.possefoundation.org/about-posse (accessed July 9, 2021).

5. Gerrelyn Patterson, "A Historically Black High School Remains Intact: We Weren't Thinking about White Students," in *School Desegregation*, ed. George W. Noblit (Boston: Sense, 2015), 63–78.

6. Jonathan Veitch and Jacques Lesure, "A Joint Statement from President Veitch and ASOC President Jacques Lesure," April 11, 2019, Occidental College Equity and Justice website, https://www.oxy.edu/about-oxy/equity-justice/community-messages/joint-statement-president-veitch-and-asoc-president; Dick Anderson, ed., "Springing into Action: Conversation Replaces Confrontation as the College Re-examines Its Commitment to Racial Equality and a Host of Other Hot-Button Issues," *Occidental Magazine*, Spring 2019, https://www.oxy.edu/magazine/issues/spring-2019/springing-action. BIPOC is an acronym for Black, Indigenous, and People of Color.

7. IAF: Industrial Areas Foundation, "Who We Are," https://www.industrialareasfoundation.org (accessed July 9, 2021); The Algebra Project, https://algebra.org/wp/ (accessed July 9, 2021); The Young People's Project, https://www.typp.org (accessed July 9, 2021).

8. USC Center for Diversity and Democracy in Partnership with CASA 0101, "Boyle Heights Museum," https://www.boyleheightsmuseum.org (accessed July 9, 2021).

9. Sokamba, "Sokamba Creative Collective," https://www.sokamba.com (accessed July 11, 2021).

10. We the People National Alliance, "Welcome to We the People National Alliance," https://mathliteracyforall.org (accessed July 11, 2021).

11. Some of this work is documented in Maria Avila, *Transformative Civic Engagement through Community Organizing* (Sterling, VA: Stylus, 2018).

6

Reimagining Civic Engagement and Academia

Joanna B. Perez and Sarah R. Taylor

Authors' Background

I met Joanna at a summer, campus-wide retreat in Lake Arrowhead in her early years at CSUDH. We met after the retreat to learn more about each other. In this meeting, she shared about her interest in working on immigration-related issues as a sociologist, and about her commitment to students whose immigrant backgrounds may present unique challenges in their academic performance. When I created the Imagining America Faculty Learning Community (FLC), I invited her to join. She was always curious about the themes we were discussing and ready to share stories about her teaching. Through this and other interactions we developed a meaningful relationship that has continued beyond the FLC.

I met Sarah at an event put together by CSUDH's Service-Learning, Internships, and Civic Engagement (SLICE) while she was presenting a poster about her research in Mexico and Central America. I was so impressed with her international civically engaged scholarship that I kept our conversation going for a good while, both of us whispering in the back, trying not to interrupt the event's speakers and presentations. Looking back, I realize part of my interest had to do with my Mexican background, but I also had a myriad of questions going through my mind about how Sarah had found her way to doing international work. I figured one way to continue to learn about her and her work would be through a collaborative project such as the FLC, so I invited her to join. We collaborated again in a second FLC, and through these two interactions I got to know her personally and professionally.

—Maria Avila

This project aligned with Imagining America (IA), an interdisciplinary and interinstitutional consortium that seeks to bring together artists, organizers, and academics to promote civic engagement, with an emphasis on arts, humanities, and design. Maria Avila has been a member of the group for many years, first learning of it through her community organizing work. In 2018 Avila brought the mission of IA to the CSUDH campus through the development of the Imagining America Faculty Learning Community (FLC), funded by the CSUDH Faculty Development Center. Through this project, a diverse group of faculty from across the campus came together to think about and imagine ways we could integrate civic engagement into our pedagogy while creating a space for a more collaborative culture on our campus. This included emphasizing the power of our personal narratives to align with IA's commitment: "We envision a world of expansive social imagination, constructed by multiple ways of knowing, where people work together to nurture healthy, vibrant, and joyful communities."[1] As we embarked on this book project, we reflected on the ways in which research in action and narrative inquiry may have the potential to create the kind of collaborative leadership we imagine by (1) creating spaces where participants can engage in conversations; (2) reflecting on how the process of collaboration and cocreation involves a period of uncertainty; (3) evolving trust in each other and identifying what each participant brings to the process; and (4) creating culture change in our institutions and communities.

The authors of this chapter, Joanna B. Perez and Sarah R. Taylor, were two of the participants in the FLC. In this chapter, we discuss the structure and deliverables of the IA FLC, but we also emphasize the lessons we learned and how we have carried these lessons into other aspects of our work as teacher-scholars. First, we position ourselves by sharing stories from our personal narratives that speak to our own higher education journeys and the funds of knowledge we draw from. The concept of "funds of knowledge" recognizes the importance of lived experience through family, household, and community interactions that learners bring to their formal education.[2] Next, we detail the collaborative nature of the IA FLC and outline the specific projects we worked on. We then go on to discuss the lessons learned through the process and reflect on the degree to which we achieved the goals of the IA FLC. Finally, we share reflections on how participating in the IA FLC prepared us for this moment, specifically the COVID-19 pandemic and antiracist movement, and their influence on our teaching, research, and scholarship. The chapter ends with a proposal to reimagine academia by integrating cross-campus collaborations among faculty and recognizing the value of civically engaged scholarship.

Positionality

Positionality refers to the idea that our personal narratives, values, and experiences shape how we see and understand the world. When using the narrative inquiry approach, it is important that we think through our positionalities and what they mean for our path to this context of higher education.

Joanna: My higher education journey is grounded on my experience as a first-generation student and proud daughter of Guatemalan immigrant parents. On their arrival to the United States, my parents were undocumented immigrants, unfamiliar with the English language, working multiple jobs to make ends meet, and navigating a new country with limited formal education. Because of the many challenges they faced, my parents always instilled in me the importance of education. I remember that from a young age, my parents would share stories about their lives in Guatemala and how they compared to their lives in California. Often, they would share how hard they had to work and how life would have perhaps been different if they would have finished their schooling. In fact, whenever I was struggling in school and was feeling unmotivated, they would remind me, "*Piensa en todos los niños en Guatemala que desean poder ir a la escuela pero no pueden porque son pobres y tienen que trabajar para ayudar a su familia. Recuerda que es un privilegio estar aquí [en los Estados Unidos] y que tu educación es inmensamente importante. Después de todo, esa es la razón porque venimos a este país, para que vos tuvieras mejores oportunidades y así no tuvieras que trabajar tan duro como nosotros para ganarse la vida.*" (Think about all the kids in Guatemala who wished they could go to school but can't because they are poor, and they have to work to help their families. Remember it is a privilege to be here [in the United States] and that your education is super important. After all, that's the reason we came to this country, for you to have better opportunities so that you do not have to work as hard as us to make a living.) To this day, my mother's words of wisdom are what keeps me grounded: "*échale ganas al estudio porque la educación es muy valioso, algo que nadie te puede quitar*" (keep up with your studies because education is really valuable, it is something that no one can take away from you).

To honor my parents' sacrifices, I took advantage of all the opportunities that would prepare me to embark on my higher education journey. Though I confronted a variety of obstacles along the way, I found joy, passion, and purpose in learning about my community through a sociological lens. Sociology is broadly defined as the study of society. Sociologists seek to critically understand the human experience by accounting for the various social processes, structures, and forces that exist in society, across time and space. In the process, sociologists conduct empirical scholarship that can inform critical social issues, deconstruct inequalities, and promote social change. In my case, sociology gave me the tools to critically analyze and contextualize my lived experiences, particularly when I learned about the sociological imagination, which is the connection between history and biography (self and society).[3] In fact, as I reflect on my participation in the FLC, I feel like this process demonstrates that it is important to learn that our narratives matter, that our experiences are important for us to understand notions of social justice and ways that we can be part of creating social change.

Besides learning how to use sociology to examine social issues, I saw the power of praxis while working at the University of California, Los Angeles (UCLA) Labor Center through my involvement with various community advocacy efforts focused on providing labor, immigration, and education rights for all. These experiences ignited my desire to become a sociology professor. Today, I am an associate professor in the Department of Sociology at CSUDH, where I get to advocate for social justice through my research, teaching, and service. My research lies at the intersection of immigration, family, education, and social movements, particularly focusing on the experiences of Latino undocumented immigrants. As a professor at a minority-serving institution, I actively aim to facilitate a student-centered learning environment and intentionally work closely with colleagues, on and off campus, to address the needs of underserved communities. It is through the exchanges I have with students, colleagues, and community partners that I remain inspired to keep doing the work that

I do. In sum, my personal experience is very much what drives the work that I do, my passion for social justice is what gives me hope for a better tomorrow, regardless of whether the work gets recognition or not. I see my work as liberating. This is why I went into academia in the first place.

Sarah: I am an associate professor in the Department of Anthropology at CSUDH. I was excited about the challenge that participating in this FLC posed for me. My research is on how Indigenous farmers are adapting their lives to take part in the tourism trade in rural Yucatán, Mexico. Before joining this FLC, I had never considered what my personal narrative had to do with my ultimate work in academia. My upbringing in a suburban Southern California environment and my research setting, which is a small Indigenous Maya village in Mexico, could not be more different from each other. To find these connections I had to think more broadly about my upbringing and the lessons I brought with me into adulthood and academia.

I had the privilege of having parents who encouraged me to have adventures and do things differently. They instilled in me that people and their stories are important, and that everyone has a story to tell. This was always something particularly important to my dad, who had studied anthropology in college. He encouraged us by saying things like "You should talk to people and find out what they're doing and have big talks with people. Don't just ask them what they do for work or how they're doing today. Ask them big questions, like what do they want to do with their lives?" Their inherent interest in the world and support of my learning really drove me to want to find the most culturally different experience that I could. I just sought it out, inside of school and outside of school, and tried to find that different experience. Ultimately, I landed in this small village for my research, and what I found that is really fascinating is that people there have amazing stories just like all people everywhere. What I've loved about it is that while there are drastic differences between my lifestyle here and my days in the field, they're also so much the same.

What they share are the mundane moments that make up a life, like conversations over meals, interactions with neighbors, and family dynamics. I think that a lot of the connection between my personal narrative and my research is just recognizing the role of culture in our lives and what a human experience all of this is, as opposed to being an American experience, or a white experience, or a Maya experience, or a Mexican experience. It's just this very human condition, so that's the connection I see.

FLC: Collaborations and Community Engagement

Our FLC was interdisciplinary, composed of faculty across disciplines. The participants came from social work, Chicana/Chicano studies, psychology, information systems, management, school leadership, sociology, labor studies, anthropology, and art and design. As a collaborative, we were interested in learning how to enhance our curriculum by incorporating civic engagement connected to the arts, humanities, or design. The IA FLC provided a space where we felt comfortable to learn, to ask questions, to reimagine, and to grow. From the beginning, Maria, as the project lead, utilized her community organizing expertise to facilitate a space that felt communal and equal across the board, irrespective of people's positionality, rank, and expertise. Through our check-ins, we began to share more about our lives within and outside of academia. We engaged in deep discussions about how we define, interpret, and apply community engagement in our scholarship, teaching, and service. And as we discussed our respective projects, we provided each other feedback and support. Hence, through a series of conversations, reflection activities, and writing sessions, we developed a sense of community and began to reimagine what was possible in the classroom, in our respective departments, and across our campus. In the process, we built on each other's strengths and began to connect on a deeper level. To this day, many of us continue to stay connected, not because we happen to work at the same institution but because we genuinely care for each other and desire to replicate our experience across campus.

During the academic year, we gathered to work through our ideas; discuss the meaning, purpose, and significance of civic engagement (or as others in the group refer to it, community engagement); and provide feedback on each other's deliverables. As a result, we were intentional about critically approaching our relationship with community partners, reshaping our teaching goals, and redefining the meaning of accomplishment. In essence, for many of us, we were experiencing a sense of collaborative learning about our work and each other for the first time. While at the time we did not know how to name this process, through this book project we now realize that we were engaging in narrative inquiry and research in action with the intention of building a collective leadership on our campus and among our communities. For instance, we would start meetings by checking in about personal stories, about our progress in integrating arts, humanities, or design into our teaching, and about exploring ways in which we could learn from each other. It was during these collaborative moments where each of us began to develop a genuine and deep appreciation for each other, not only in terms of our work and our role as professors but also as human beings invested in creating social change.

IA FLC Deliverables: Individual Projects and Faculty Reflections

In this section we reflect about courses in our respective disciplines in which we integrated community engagement projects related to arts and humanities.

Immigrant Photo Essays and Community Exhibit

Joanna: As a community-engaged scholar and student-centered professor, I am invested in facilitating learning environments where students recognize their brilliance, resilience, and potential to create social change in their respective communities. I often remind students that their narrative matters and that they are knowledge producers because I want them to realize that they play an equal role in helping everyone in the classroom understand the course content through their narrative, personal experiences, and funds of knowledge. This is especially important to me because the majority are first-generation, low-income students of color who are often marginalized in the larger society. As such, for my FLC project, I sought to integrate civic engagement and the arts in my first-year seminar, Undocumented and Unafraid.

On our campus, first-year seminars are part of the Dominguez Hills First Year Experience initiative, which aims to promote student success by enriching the educational experience of freshmen students through culturally responsive and high-impact practices. Culturally responsive practices draw on the "cultural knowledge, prior experiences, frames of reference, and performance styles of ethnically diverse students to make learning encounters more relevant to and effective for them."[4] High-impact practices (HIPs) are generally "time-intensive academic pursuits that provide structured opportunities for meaningful interactions with faculty and peers regarding course-related topics as well as positive interactions with others from diverse backgrounds."[5] Both culturally responsive and high-impact practices promote academic success among underserved student populations. In fact, research shows that these culturally responsive practices are instrumental for the psychological well-being of students of color, who represent the largest demographic on our campus.[6] Hence, in addition to implementing these practices, first-year seminars are designed to help freshmen students build meaningful relationships with their peers and mentoring relationships with their professors so that they gain a sense of belonging and increase their likelihood of completing their degrees.

In *Undocumented and Unafraid*, I introduce students to sociological concepts, theories, and research methods to analyze immigration in the United States. In order to enhance their sociological imagination, students work on a final project throughout the semester where they analyze how history, social structures, law, and culture impact the daily lives of immigrants. First, students write a poem based on their perception of undocumented immigrants, as portrayed in the larger society. Once all students complete the poem, we carve out time in class to discuss the social construction of immigration, which includes analyzing our own social position based on our intersectional identity. Second, students interview an immigrant they admire, which often ends up being a family member, neighbor, friend, or someone on campus. Through this interview, students become familiar with the migration journey, sacrifices, challenges, changes, and unique experiences that their interviewee undergoes on arrival in the United States. By the end of the interview, students learn about the immigrant's past, their experience while living in the United States, and personal reflections on today's political climate. Third, the students learn how to transcribe, code, and analyze interview data. The students then complete a brainstorming handout in order to delineate their final project topic, three main themes, social position of the interviewee, and the ways that the larger society including historical as well as structural forces impact their lives. To introduce students how to utilize campus resources, I then have students attend a library session to learn about library resources useful for research, including learning how to find academic sources and properly cite. By the end of the session, students are prepared to proceed with the next step, which is to write an annotated bibliography. To enhance their writing and critical thinking skills, students then write a final paper outline, on which I provide extensive feedback. Before proceeding with writing their final paper, students take photographs of their interviewee in order to provide a visual context of their lives. Students then integrate their research through a photo essay.

On completing their final paper, students present their work to the class, and I also organize a campus photo exhibit that features their work, which is open to the campus community as well as the students' family and loved ones. While the event aims to amplify and celebrate the work of the students, it also provides them with the unique opportunity of having their family and loved ones come to campus, often for the first time. Given that the majority of my students are children of immigrants and/or part of a mixed-status family, the photo exhibit helps them witness how despite their social position, they are knowledge bearers and have actively taken part in acknowledging the resiliency of immigrants in our society. At the same time, their families are able to feel part of the CSUDH community and recognize the important role they play in the educational aspirations and achievements of their students. The sense of community and family among us is deeply moving and demonstrates not only the power of praxis but also the transformational potential that we have when we create a safe space that welcomes those who are instrumental in the lives of our students.

Given the success of the campus photo exhibit, my work during my participation in the FLC sought to enhance the final project and event by reconceptualizing the meaning of community and integrating civic engagement. More specifically, rather than only regarding people and organizations outside of campus as "community partners," we looked within our campus to start the community engagement. As such, students worked alongside our community partner, the Toro Dreamers Success Center (TDSC), and then branched out to become familiar with immigrant rights organizations. What they found was that often immigrants, including the families and loved ones of students, do not utilize the resources and services of immigrant rights organizations because they were unaware, intimidated, or afraid. Therefore, we decided to use the photo exhibit event as a bridge between community organizations and immigrant families by hosting a resource fair. In the end, the resource fair consisted of the Central American Resource Center (CARECEN), APLA Health, Mexican American Opportunity Foundation (MAOF), and the Coalition for Humane Immigrant Rights Los Angeles (CHIRLA). Attendees of the campus photo exhibit became familiar with the services and resources available to immigrants, including free legal aid, a health program, help with filing taxes, and overall support for immigrant rights. At the same time, we also invited campus organizations that promote the support for undocumented students and students in mixed-status families, including Espiritu de Nuestro Futuro (ENF): Immigrant Student Alliance, Undocumented Student Ally Coalition (USAC), and the larger CSUDH community. In the end, this student-led and community-centered civically engaged endeavor demonstrated the power of reimagining the ways in which we conceptualize and contextualize civic engagement in and outside of the classroom and how we can use the arts and humanities to acknowledge, validate, and affirm the stories and voices of marginalized communities, particularly immigrants.

Ethnographic Service Learning and Civic Engagement

Sarah: As part of the IA Faculty Learning Community, I selected an existing assignment from the applied anthropology course that I teach every fall semester. For this assignment, students work individually in the first half of the semester to document their observations of life at CSUDH by writing field notes. After the midterm exam, we work together to refine their observations into four project ideas that the students can work on. They spend the remainder of the semester conducting a needs assessment on this topic, and they present their findings at the end. Their performance on this project is assessed using rubrics for their individual field notes, group participation, and final presentations.

I emphasize three key skills in this course: oral presentation, competence with creating posters, and interpersonal and team interaction skills. The final step in the service learning project is a report on their findings. They present their research in poster format on the last day of class. Throughout the semester, students work on a variety of tasks with their peers in two different groups. This format gives them important experience and builds their interpersonal skills.

While this assignment has been effective, I was enthusiastic about the prospect of revising it to meet the FLC's call for publicly engaged scholarship that integrates student learning with the needs of community partners. This assignment was prime for revision because, while the class is designated as a service learning course, the assignment specifically did not meet the basic criteria for service learning.

Service learning promotes learning experiences through student volunteerism and engagement with community partners and allows for the application of student knowledge.[7] Sanday and Jannowitz suggest "that anthropology is uniquely relevant to the educative function of community service learning because of the role the concept of culture plays in the development of multiculturally-sensitive citizens."[8] In researching this intersection of anthropology and service learning pedagogy, I found the concept of ethnographic service learning. Ethnographic service learning is achieved by conducting ethnographic projects based on the service learning model.[9] This model has a number of benefits. Perhaps the most important for the context of this FLC is that it highlights the integration of the humanistic and scientific sides of anthropology.

In terms of civic engagement, this assignment had great potential. The needs assessment methods are concrete, empirical methods that students use for data collection in a short period; however, in its previous iteration the assignment was not yielding meaningful civic engagement. I had developed the previous student learning outcomes (SLOs) to connect the course to disciplinary curriculum. By the end of the course, students would be able to (1) understand the relationship between key concepts in anthropology and their application to human problems; (2) identify the unique ethical challenges that applied anthropologists face; and (3) employ critical thinking to predict potentials for applied anthropology in the world. The first two SLOs are about theoretical comprehension of applied anthropology, and the third is a broader critical-thinking outcome. These are appropriate SLOs for a typical applied anthropology course, but participating in the IA FLC drove me to learn about the types of SLOs common in community-engaged courses. Medeiros and Guzmán suggest five ideal SLOs for meaningful ethnographic service learning: (1) theoretical comprehension; (2) engagement with community partners; (3) skills training; (4) reflection; and (5) dissemination of findings.[10]

The literature on needs assessment identifies a variety of types of need.[11] These include felt needs and expressed needs. The needs assessment of the campus community was a useful assignment; however, because students are also members of this community, they rarely moved from identifying felt needs to actually assessing expressed needs. By moving the assignment to engagement with community partners, students have to ask people what the needs are (expressed needs) and are not able to rely on their own perception of what the needs may be (felt needs). The fact that they are engaging with local community partners creates a learning relationship between students and community partners and alleviates the common "otherizing" found in student research.[12] The revised SLOs are to

(1) Understand the relationship between key concepts in anthropology and their application to human problems;

(2) Engage in an ethnographic needs assessment based on issues identified by community partners;

(3) Utilize methods from applied anthropology in design and execution of needs assessment;

(4) Reflect on connections between work for community partners and concepts of applied anthropology; and

(5) Deliver useful content to community partners depending on results of needs assessment (survey data, promotional materials, outreach results, etc.) and present results to campus community.

As part of the community-based needs assessment, students now must engage with a variety of people instead of just fellow students. I have taught the class twice since the revision, and the difference in the research students undertake is notable. Both years students have continued with an on-campus needs assessment, but they now have to engage with stakeholders from across campus (as opposed to only fellow students). I am also a part of an FLC that was an outgrowth of the IA FLC focused on integrating community engagement in general education (see chapter 7 in this book). Students in my applied class have conducted their needs assessment to contribute to the work of that group. I find that they are more committed to the research projects because they see a role for them beyond simply earning a grade. Students report that they enjoyed being a part of something that would last beyond just the semester. An additional requirement is to report their findings to the campus community. In spring 2020 a group from the previous semester's applied anthropology course made a presentation of their needs assessment on the feasibility of a community engagement minor to the Community Engagement in General Education FLC. All groups are also expected to present their research to the campus community during Student Research Day, an annual campus-wide event where students are mentored by faculty to present their research projects.

Engaging with Faculty, Students, and Community Partners

A highlight of participating in this FLC was the space we created where we could collaborate, learn, and cocreate new ways of doing our civically engaged scholarship through our teaching and/or research. During our last meeting, others expressed similar reflective comments, including one participant who managed to develop a new community engagement course for her department after participating in the FLC. In the final report, various participants reflected on their experience, including this comment from Joanna: "This has truly been an amazing and transformational experience for me. . . . While being involved in FLC, I have gained the confidence of implementing civic engagement in my course [and] beyond the classroom space. I have been able to build close relationships with campus entities [and] community organizations. I have learned a lot through all my colleagues in the FLC [which have] inspired me to keep doing the work that I have always wanted to do."

In sum, beyond implementing civic engagement in our classes, participating in the FLC provided us with the space to recognize the importance of community. By collaborating with faculty across disciplines, we grew as teacher-scholars and learned best practices to approach faculty, students, and community partners in a meaningful and collaborative manner. On reflection, we propose that others also implement the following best practices: (1) take the time to build rapport (humanize the interaction by learning about each other); (2) be open to sharing and drawing from our positionality (recognize the power of our narrative and funds of knowledge); (3) build common ground to create a plan of action (use shared interests, passions, strengths, and goals); (4) follow up and support (conduct regular check-ins and be open to learning from each other by providing critical feedback throughout the process). When these best practices are used with both folks on campus and noncampus groups, community engagement is not only possible but also transformational. This means that rather than seeing our interactions with others as transactional, we treat them as reciprocal, where both parties are respected, honored, and uplifted.

The Utility of Narrative Inquiry

Narrative inquiry is important to all of the projects discussed in this book, but we think it is particularly useful in understanding this FLC that was linked to Imaging America. When you review the organization's goals and missions, you see that the idea underlying them is that we really have to hear peoples' stories to think about ways we can reimagine together, so that we can integrate humanities and design into various aspects of higher education. That is exactly what happened during the course of this work together in the IA FLC.

Pedagogical Approach and Campus Community

Joanna: Through narrative inquiry, I was not only able to enhance my pedagogical approach; I was also able to build meaningful relationships with everyone in the IA FLC. This gave me the opportunity to build a strong community of colleagues across disciplines by learning about their educational journeys, strategies to initiate relationships with community partners, and the unique ways to implement community-engaged curriculum in their teaching. Through this exchange, I came out learning more about them, myself, and the ways that I could transform my own work, especially within and outside of the classroom.

Tenets of Education and Teaching

Sarah: For me, this was the first time I had an opportunity to spend time with professors from across campus and really talk about the tenets of education and the way we educate students in a way that was unattached to my disciplinary expertise. We were not talking about how to teach anthropology; we were spending time sharing ideas about how to teach. We got to hear each other's stories and think about what they do in the classroom, what they do out of the classroom, and really who they are. The inclusion of all of our personal narratives influenced the way I experienced the FLC and also shaped the way I integrated it into my teaching.

IA FLC Prepared Us for This Moment: Responding to COVID-19 and the Anti-Racist Movement

In 2020 we began to live under unique circumstances due to the COVID-19 global pandemic, which altered the way we approach our teaching, research, and service. For many of us, it meant learning how to teach online for the first time, and more importantly, practicing compassion and flexibility with our students and ourselves. For instance, we have had to learn how to cope with extraneous and tragic challenges related to the pandemic, including accessibility (digital divide), inadequate learning/teaching environment, social isolation, financial hardship (unemployment, housing and/or food insecurity), added home responsibilities (caring for siblings, children, elderly parents, etc.), health inequities, and grieving the loss of loved ones. Also, we are living in a time when the world is witnessing a collective awakening to racial injustice, white supremacy, police violence, and systemic racism, particularly due to the anti-racist efforts of the Black Lives Matter movement. And in thinking about the students and communities we serve, we found ourselves managing the anxiety, fear, and stress related to the US presidential election, the legal limbo experienced because of the Deferred Action for Childhood Arrivals (DACA) decision, and the impact of global warming and natural disasters. To this end, these unforeseen circumstances have impacted how we engage with each other in all areas of our lives, what and how we teach, how we continue our research virtually, and how we use our service commitments to continue to promote social change.

Joanna: As a sociology professor, I am constantly thinking about the best ways to create a learning environment where students are able to not only learn but also reflect on the ways in which social issues impact their daily lives. In the process, keeping in mind my own positionality and the unique experiences of the students we serve at CSUDH, I attempt to use my platform in the classroom as an opportunity to help students recognize their resilience and power in creating social change. Hence, as I witnessed the growing challenges my students and my community were facing due to the pandemic and the impact of the Black Lives Matter movement, the immigrant rights movement, and other uprisings tied to social justice issues, I knew that I had to make changes in my curriculum. Besides being more intentional about centering the narratives and experiences of people of color (POC) through my selection of readings (authored predominantly by POC), I also created more student-centered assignments so that students had the space to reflect on their current life situations. More importantly, it was crucial to prioritize my students' mental health and well-being. This meant taking the time to do more check-ins with them than I would normally do during a regular semester, motivating them to be transparent, and figuring out how we can support each other. It was these moments that allowed us to create a sense of community virtually, because as we shared, we got to know each other better, validate our emotions, and make sense of what we were going through. This allowed us to feel more connected and united even though we were socially/physically distant from one another.

After teaching online for the first time in the fall 2020 semester, I have found that now more than ever, what we teach, how we teach, and our assessment process must align with notions of social justice, equity, and community building. And while civic/community engagement may look different virtually, having students apply what they learn outside of our online sessions continues to be central in my classes. Hence, in my Undocumented and Unafraid course, first-year students continue to conduct their final project focused on immigration, but rather than having a photo exhibit, students are creating and sharing videos related to their research and interview analysis with community partners. In exchange, community partners share their expertise and experiences with students during virtual convenings.

In addition to making changes in my teaching, I have also had to rethink how I approach my research. While research is a large part of our work as professors, the current situation has pushed me to think more broadly about what research looks like virtually and how I can continue to use my research expertise to address the issues at hand. In my case, my work on Latino undocumented immigrant activists continues, but in my analysis, I am more intentional about incorporating an intersectional lens to contextualize and make connections between their lived experiences and that of other marginalized communities suffering from injustice. For instance, I aim to contextualize the ways that immigrants and POC fight against systemic racism and structural inequality, whether it be by fighting against deportations, the expansion of detention centers, police brutality, racial profiling, or injustices within the prison-industrial complex. Also, in an effort to bridge my research to the work of grassroots organizers, I have become involved with more community-engaged research, like the UndocuScholars project, where I collaborate with undocumented students and allies to understand the implications that the current political climate has on the lives of undocumented immigrants. In other words, I am using strategies that capitalize on the strengths of both the researchers and the participants so that we can cocreate a project that is meaningful for everyone. Through these efforts, I have witnessed the importance of taking a more community-based approach to research.

Besides my teaching and scholarship, the COVID-19 pandemic and the anti-racist movement have also motivated me to remain engaged in service opportunities that aim to address the needs of underserved students. Through my department and disciplinary service, I continue to ensure that sociology students are getting the support they need to thrive academically and be prepared to tackle larger social issues in their respective communities. Given the instrumental role that mentors play in my life, I continue to mentor several students through the McNair Scholars Program, independent study, and assistance in applying to graduate school. I also continue to be an advocate for undocumented students through my involvement with the Undocumented Student Ally Coalition and the Toro Dreamers Success Center, which includes but is not limited to hosting virtual events and programing, and offering opportunities to enhance their academic and professional experience as well as promote their well-being (i.e., mental health). More recently, I became part of the First-Generation Program committee, which focuses on providing first-generation students support through workshops, events, and mentorship. In all the aforementioned service commitments, I have deeply appreciated and gained a lot from having conversations with faculty, staff, and administrators. Together, we have discussed the ways our students are being impacted by the pandemic and a wide range of social injustices around the world, and how we can play a role in helping students cope and remain empowered to press forward. Ultimately, this has shown me the great potential we have as an institution to promote access, equity, and social justice.

Sarah: The moment we are living through—a time of pandemic, social uprisings, and political uncertainty—has led to a need to reconcile our teaching, research, and social engagements. We went through all these trainings in the summer of 2020 to find ways to hold it all together and make it work, but there has to be a recognition that this is not normal. This is not, like, "I'm going to teach online now and so I have to learn how to teach online." There's no class to learn how to teach from my bedroom. This is an unprecedented time, and it is really beautiful to think about having that kind of grace, not just for our students but for ourselves as well. My teaching obviously has changed a lot due to the transition to online learning, but it has been really impacted more so than any other area by the Black Lives Matter movement and the uprisings of summer 2020. This forced me to really be intentional about talking about what I'm teaching and including my perspective. I realized that I have this cushion to fall back on because I'm an anthropologist, so, of course, I'm thinking about social justice and equity, and diversity. But the reality is, if you're not talking about it and being really explicit about its role in your research and in your scholarship and in your teaching, then it doesn't actually matter. It is the difference between talking about social justice in lectures and letting it inform your teaching in meaningful ways. I had to reckon with myself this summer and think about how to make that change. I revised my syllabus for Introduction to Cultural Anthropology, which is the biggest class I teach. I teach two sections a semester, a total of about eighty students. This process made me think critically about the history of our discipline.

Early anthropology started as a colonial endeavor. The idea was, "If we understand these savages we can better govern them," and with that, some of the earliest anthropologists conducted their research under the auspices of colonial government positions. That is, of course, not the case in our discipline now, but it matters a lot that we are open about that and clear with our students. I think it especially matters to our students at CSUDH, and that's where some of the upper-division kind of revisions that I have had to make come in. I tell my students that anthropology is for everyone and that there are lots of ways they can apply it in the workplace. I am very much a cheerleader for it, but I am standing up here as the traditional anthropologist. I am a white woman and I go off to a tiny Indigenous village and I sleep in a hammock and do these very stereotypical anthropological things, but I am telling them that not all anthropologists are like this even though all the people you're learning from are. Because of this realization, I have done a lot of work to diversify who they are reading and learning from, so it is not just my voice but also those of others. Through this process, I learned something really interesting. I knew who Zora Neale Hurston was, of course. I was very aware of her and her research and that she was a contemporary of Margaret Mead. What I did not know until the summer of 2020 was that she wrote a book in 1931, an oral history of one of the last known survivors of the last slave ship called *Barracoon: The Story of the Last "Black Cargo."*[13] Apparently, publishers were very excited about it, but when they got the final version they wanted her to change it from the dialect that her collaborator was speaking to standard English. She refused to do it, and so they refused to publish it. Learning that was really an important moment for me and kind of shifted my ideas about what I wanted my students to know about anthropology, and it has forced me to be more explicit about my own positionality. I think that there is a different connection when I tell students, "As I'm saying these words to you about how anybody can do anthropology, I know that I am a white person who goes off to this tiny Indigenous village, but this is not all of our discipline." I feel like saying those words explicitly has changed what my students think is appropriate to talk about in the classroom. We have had some really good conversations.

In terms of my scholarship, it is really hard to do my kind of research online. I obviously cannot travel to Mexico, and this is the longest I have been away from Mexico since 2004. I am doing other types of work there by coordinating aid efforts with other nonprofits who have worked in the community and leveraging the fact that they are all in Mexico. They have all of these volunteers who have come through over the years—college students doing their social service requirement—and my past students oftentimes have greater means to contribute more, so we have been collecting donations to buy corn and various things. COVID-19 has of course been really detrimental to a tourism economy, which is what that village runs on. Then two hurricanes came through so they are really suffering a lot—they lost what was left of their harvest for the year. It is not scholarship, per se, but it feels really linked to my scholarship because it is this place that has been kind enough to let me study there.

Reimagining Academia: Collaborations and Culture Shift

Through this reflection about the IA FLC, we have reimagined and redefined our roles as professors, scholars, and community-engaged activists. More broadly, we have reimagined academia as a whole because rather than continuing to normalize and perpetuate notions of individualism and meritocracy, we now actively work toward finding ways and spaces to collaborate and to value the work that we do within and outside of academia. When we think about where we started and where we are today, we feel inspired and rejuvenated because we can confidently say that we are part of a collective that values and promotes civically engaged teaching, scholarship, and service. Key to these efforts is continuing to work across disciplines so that faculty, students, staff, and administrators can all benefit from this culture shift.

> *Joanna:* Counter to the egocentric and competitive nature of academia, my parents' teachings of humility, community, and service are what shapes my evolvement as professor and community-engaged scholar. For instance, my parents have always instilled in me the importance of humility. One of the prime examples that continues to shape my understanding of humility was when my parents told me, "*no importa tu educación o experiencia, recorda que siempre podes aprender algo de otros*" (no matter your education or experience, remember you can always learn something from others). This means realizing that I am a lifelong learner and that I have much to gain from all whom I encounter, including students, colleagues, community partners, and community members. In other words, rather than entering any situation as an expert, I enter as a colearner, which grants me the ability to listen attentively and build meaningful relationships with others. Besides aiming to embody humility, my parents' teachings about the value of community and my responsibility to be of service to anyone in need are what continues to guide my efforts to provide an alternative narrative to what is possible in academia. It is through this process that I get to constantly redefine my position and purpose in academe.

As I reflect on my own trajectory, I find that to promote a culture shift in academia, we must carefully and intentionally account for our funds of knowledge and our positionality, and be open to reflection, growth, and collaboration. Rather than abiding to meritocracy and a deficit mindset, this requires that we take action to acknowledge, validate, and uplift the narratives and strengths of our students, campus community, and surrounding communities. Through this process, we can implement strategies that promote equity within and beyond college campuses.

Sarah: As I mentioned, my father studied anthropology in college, and he is a great example of that idea that you have a story that may or may not be related to what you do for a living. He has a college degree in anthropology and religious studies, and he ended up with a career working in a lumberyard. His attitude was always that college teaches you how to learn things, so it does not really matter what you study. You should study whatever you love because what you are learning is how to learn, how to function, and how to deal with people. So, he worked in a totally unrelated field—definitely not an anthropologist or anything related to it—but in his life he lived that example of people having stories that are more than what you see on the surface. I bring this perspective to my teaching, and especially in the general education courses I teach.

As we reflect on our funds of knowledge, higher education journeys, experience within the IA FLC, and the ways in which we are approaching our role as teacher-scholars, we recognize that now more than ever we need to continue to do the work to reimaging academia. It is time we interrogate what the role of academia is in our democratic society, and prioritizing civically engaged scholarship and pedagogy is an important step in the process. We regularly assess our curriculum and think about why certain classes need to be included to convey specific ideas, but thinking about civic engagement in higher education more broadly is a chance for us to examine the value of an education. Finally, having witnessed the power of collaborative leadership throughout our participation in the IA FLC and this book project, we aim to implement these same strategies within our respective departments and across campus. While collaborative leadership may take more time and effort, we know that it has the power to transform the academy and the larger society.

Notes

1. Imagining America: Artists and Scholars in Public Life, "Mission," https://imaginingamerica.org/who-we-are/we-envision/ (accessed February 22, 2022).

2. Norma González, Luis C. Moll, and Cathy Amanti, *Funds of Knowledge: Theorizing Practices in Households, Communities, and Classrooms* (New York: Routledge, 2005).

3. C. Wright Mills, *Sociological Imagination* (New York: Oxford University Press, 2000).

4. Geneva Gay, *Culturally Responsive Teaching: Theory, Research, and Practice* (New York: Teachers College Press, 2000), 29.

5. Amy K. Ribera, Angie L. Miller, and Amber D. Dumford, "Sense of Peer Belonging and Institutional Acceptance in the First Year: The Role of High-Impact Practices," *Journal of College Student Development* 58, no. 4 (2017): 546.

6. Blaire Cholewa, Rachael D. Goodman, Cirecie West-Olatunji, and Ellen Amatea, "A Qualitative Examination of the Impact of Culturally Responsive Educational Practices on the Psychological Well-Being of Students of Color," *Urban Review* 46 (2014): 574–96.

7. Jean Ivey, "Service Learning Research," *Pediatric Nursing* 37, no. 2 (2011): 74–76.

8. Peggy Reeves Sanday and Karl Jannowitz, "Public Interest Anthropology: A Boasian Service-Learning Initiative," *Michigan Journal of Community Service Learning* 10, no. 3 (2004): 64–75.

9. Melanie A. Medeiros and Jennifer Guzmán, "Ethnographic Service Learning: An Approach for Transformational Learning," *Teaching Anthropology* 6 (2016): 66–72.

10. Medeiros and Guzmán, "Ethnographic Service Learning."

11. J. K. Burton and P. F. Merrill, "Needs Assessment: Goals, Needs, and Priorities," in *Instructional Design: Principles and Applications*, 2nd ed., ed. Leslie J. Briggs, Kent L. Gustafson, and Murray H. Tillman (Englewood Cliffs, NJ: Educational Technology Publications, 1991), 17–43.

12. Sam Beck, "Community Service Learning: A Model for Teaching and Activism," *North American Dialog* 9 (2006): 1–7.

13. Zora Neale Hurston, *Barracoon: The Story of the Last "Black Cargo"* (New York: Amistad, 2018).

7

Integrating Civic Engagement into General Education at California State University, Dominguez Hills

Philip A. Vieira, Xuefei Deng, and Gabrielle Seiwert

Authors' Background

I met Philip at the same summer campus-wide retreat where I met Joanna. While we did not have an opportunity to interact then, I remember being struck by his comments about his interest in collaborative work. At the time, I was chair of the Academic Senate Faculty Policy Committee, and I invited him to join as a representative of his college. We had several opportunities to interact, which is how I got to know more about his research interests, especially related to exploring ways to build collaboratives, and about his work related to integrating high-impact practices in the classroom. He always seemed very thoughtful and reflective, and able to talk about himself as a person.

I met Xuefei—or Nancy, as I have known her—in the Academic Senate while I was chair of the Faculty Policy Committee, and we followed up with a meeting over coffee to learn more about each other's work. Nancy's work on issues of equity related to minority, first-generation students piqued my interest. Both Philip and Nancy were very engaged in the conversations we had as a group in this project and were able to connect their research methodologies as we explored ways to integrate community engagement into the general education curriculum.

Gabbie (as she prefers to be called informally) was invited to the group by her colleague Veronica Toledo, whom I had met as a student during my work at Occidental. They were both representing the voice of community partners in this group. Although Gabbie's experience of being in a group of mostly faculty made it difficult for her to participate at the beginning, she soon got integrated into the conversations and events related to the group. When I invited her to coauthor this chapter, I followed my email invitation with a phone meeting. In this meeting, I learned about her interest in organizing to bring equity to underrepresented students in the Los Angeles Unified School District.

—*Maria Avila*

In the fall of 2019 and the spring of 2020, Maria Avila created a research-in-action Faculty Learning Community (FLC) focused on integrating civic engagement (CE)[1] into general education (GE) courses at California State University, Dominguez Hills (CSUDH). The project emerged from a partnership between California State University, Northridge, College of the Canyons, and Cerritos College, originally funded by Bringing Theory to Practice (BT2P).[2] At CSUDH, the bulk of the funding for this FLC came from the Center for Service-Learning, Internships, and Civic Engagement (SLICE), through the office of the dean of undergraduate studies.

The project started with six faculty members from psychology, anthropology, social work, educational leadership, art, and information systems. What began as an interesting discussion about the state of community engagement on our campus and ways to institutionalize a pathway to increase student access to this type of education eventually led to an agreement to work toward creating a community engagement minor. Looking for feedback on this idea, we held a meeting where we invited members from SLICE, students, and community partners in the first semester of the project. For some of us, this was the first time we engaged in conversation with these stakeholders about community engagement. From the feedback we received at this meeting, we decided to invite members from these stakeholders to our group. We also invited a faculty member from Cerritos College (a participant of the project funded by BT2P). Thus, the group was no longer an FLC, but it continued with the collaborative format Avila had introduced us to through her research-in-action and narrative inquiry methodologies.

For some of us, this was the first time we were aware of such methodologies, although some of us had had previous experiences with collaborative projects. The authors of this chapter learned about these methodologies in the collaborative, dialogical space we were part of during the duration of the project, and we have furthered our understanding of what we learned and experienced through the writing of this chapter. The following discussion illustrates the use of a collective leadership model in a genuine partnership between stakeholders from the community and the university, providing an example for how to create room for culture change within the campus community.

Our Roles and Contributions

The authors of this chapter represent different backgrounds, including associate professor of psychology Philip Vieira, professor of information systems Xuefei Deng, and community partner Gabbie Seiwert. We share here how our backgrounds informed our individual contributions to this project and the way in which these contributions have meaning to each of us.

Philip: I am an associate professor in the Department of Psychology at CSUDH. While my primary research training is in neuropharmacology, I am also involved in other projects on our campus. Many of these projects are collaborations with colleagues in academia, but it wasn't until I participated in this project that I came to understand the impact of true collective leadership (further described below). Initial conversations about this project with Maria changed my perspective on my ongoing academic collaborations, and I decided to join her as she explored this collective leadership model in practice.

One of the projects I lead on our campus is a faculty development program for high-impact educational practices (HIPs),[3] and this work, in part, led me to join the research-in-action FLC on civic engagement. I had begun to study the impact of service learning (as an HIP) on student success and wanted to better understand efforts to broaden student participation in these activities at our campus. Additionally, I believe these practices yield benefits for the faculty who facilitate them as well as the community partners and I aim to study these relationships as well. By participating in this FLC, therefore, I hoped to learn more about the practice of civic engagement and collective leadership.

As the group began assessing the state of community engagement on our campus, we embarked on a process of inquiry about what we know and what we would like to know. This is how we found out that our campus center for civic engagement (SLICE) had done several faculty surveys in the past, and the data from these surveys led us to further questions. We designed a survey for community partners to learn about their experiences working with our campus and academic institutions more generally. We developed a second survey to inventory those faculty who have engaged with the community as part of their scholarship and/or courses. Finally, we created a third survey to help define what community engagement meant for faculty on our campus and identify challenges using CE in their work. The use of surveys is part of my own research as an experimental psychologist, and therefore my role in this project included the development and analysis of these surveys.

Xuefei: I am a professor of information systems in the College of Business Administration and Public Policy at CSUDH. I joined the FLC after Maria invited me and explained that the project would be collaborative and participatory such that a group of interested faculty members would be engaged in learning, discussing, reflecting, and making recommendations and decisions together. She also explained that the methodology of narrative inquiry is useful for creative activities and scholarship by participants sharing stories and exchanging viewpoints related to a project goal. While I am trained to conduct empirical research based on qualitative and quantitative data analysis, I'm also interested in learning and applying new methodologies such as narrative inquiry. My origin in China is central to my personal narrative. I came to the United States in 1994 to pursue my MBA and later my PhD degree in information systems. My first name is Xuefei, which means "flying snowflake." Yet due to the difficulties my American schoolmates and colleagues had in pronouncing my name, I switched to my English name "Nancy," as I was called by my American teacher back in China.

Professionally, I saw this project as an opportunity to share and contribute my academic research knowledge and skills to a teaching-oriented project that would have a good potential to make an immediate impact on our students' learning outcomes. During the project, I had the opportunity to contribute my empirical research design skills (survey design) and data analysis to the project work. In the process, I also learned from other participants with different areas of expertise and viewpoints.

My role in this project included data analysis, survey design, and administration. First, I analyzed data collected from previous surveys administered by SLICE and prepared a summary for the group about student and faculty experiences with CE activities and curriculum. Related to students' opinion and feedback, I analyzed the data from two SLICE surveys on student learning outcomes of community engagement and service learning (CE/SL). The analysis of previous surveys from SLICE has shown that both students and faculty are interested in community engagement–related learning. The insights from these data led me to work with the group to create and conduct the surveys described above. My participation in this FLC has made me appreciate the collaborative spirit and data-driven approach in a successful research-in-action project. I believe such an approach will be beneficial to promoting and sustaining the growth of institutions, organizations, and communities.

Gabbie: I am a community engagement coordinator at United Parents and Students,[4] a nonprofit organization that works with public schools and community-based organizations to empower low-income communities to advocate for the resources and services their neighborhoods need through organizing and civic engagement. In my role, I work with parents and students to identify and address obstacles to education outside school walls that not only pose barriers to learning but also inhibit local quality of life.

I was drawn to participate in this project due to my experience with community engagement during my own undergraduate education and its impact on my career trajectory. I attended Occidental College where I participated in many community-based learning classes through the Center for Community Based Learning (CCBL). Community engagement during my undergraduate education not only transformed the way I thought about education, scholarship, and service but also helped me clarify my career interests and provided me with professional connections I would have otherwise lacked. After graduating, I was able to connect with fellow Occidental College alumna Veronica Toledo, the associate director of the organization where I currently work, United Parents and Students. Veronica had also participated in CCBL courses during her time at Occidental, and our shared understanding of community engagement was a critical component of her decision to hire me for my current role. My experience in CCBL classes in college directly translated to my current role by building skills in communication, organization, and professionalism while simultaneously teaching me the importance of nonacademic knowledge and experience. I believe deeply in the benefits of community engagement and was excited at the opportunity to help strengthen those types of opportunities for college students at CSUDH.

This project also appealed to me because I have seen the transformation students who have worked with United Parents and Students have undergone as they've grown to become advocates for their families, schools, neighborhoods, and communities. I've seen how learning the power of their voices can not only impact their external environment and community but can also provide students with a chance to develop their own sense of self and build confidence and self-assurance. My coworkers and I have also benefited from the research and advocacy students have provided, as well as the new and innovative perspectives students often bring to our work. The possibility of having more avenues through which to partner with students at schools like CSUDH was incredibly appealing, and I looked forward to strengthening those opportunities.

In the FLC, my role was primarily to provide a community partner perspective in discussions of how the community engagement minor would work with community-based organizations. I worked with faculty, staff, and my own supervisor to shape and distribute a survey to community partners, which was used to gather feedback about the potential community engagement minor. Later, I also worked to help identify potential CE courses from current GE course offerings with another member of the FLC.

Collective Leadership Model

The diverse group of individual team members, which included CSUDH faculty and students, SLICE members, community partners, a faculty member from a community college, and the dean of undergraduate studies, made up the backbone of this project, bringing with them their unique backgrounds and areas of expertise to tackle a common goal together. Rather than focusing on a top-down hierarchical approach, we benefited immensely from working together to make decisions and accomplish tasks in an open and transparent manner. We strove to ensure that no voice was louder and no person carried more weight in decisions. This goal, though explicitly stated from the start of our collaboration, took time to be applied implicitly. Much of our lives, both professionally and personally, are guided by traditional approaches to leadership, a default approach to how we understand and operate in the world. When this group came together for a meeting, the individuals were often rushing from a classroom where they were leading a group of students through a lecture or preplanned activities, or their lab where student assistants follow their weekly orders, or even another meeting with colleagues, checking off agenda items prescribed by a superior. Inevitably, we would need time to shift gears from the solitary leadership world we left to join the collective leadership world of our group. The start of each meeting involved an open-forum style of sharing our current state of mind, an intentional ritual of checking in with each individual to shed some stress from the day, recognize upcoming deadlines, or even simply state a single emotion to encompass how we were feeling in that moment. Simply asking everyone, "How are you feeling right now? What draws your attention at this moment?" in an open space is a subtle but important change from how most of our interactions begin, with an exchange of the polite but often superficial pleasantries of "How are you? Great, me too." This served to shift our mindset off the default track of prior personal/professional engagements toward our collective space for sharing, and it also helped build trust between the individual members, creating a safe space to explore and attempt to realize the goals of the collective leadership model. Though we understood that these goals could never be achieved absolutely, they served as guideposts for us during our work, important reminders that our individual perspective was valued and that we each had a voice in leading this project. Every team member had some ownership of the work being done, which in turn promoted a deeper and more creative engagement in the process.

While collective leadership has grown in popularity in the corporate world, even spawning popular applications like Slack and Microsoft Teams, this model of shared governance has lagged in academic adoption. The project described in this chapter serves as a model for how to implement collective leadership with multiple stakeholders in higher education. Below, the individual authors describe their individual experience with this model.

Philip: At first glance, *collective leadership* may sound oxymoronic: *leadership* implies a hierarchy, with one unit at the top and following subunits beneath. Certainly, my own experience in academia has provided few examples of collective leadership. From kindergarten to my PhD, classrooms, clubs, teams, and laboratories all functioned on a traditional leadership model, with a leader (class president, team captain, principal investigator) at the top and subordinates below. On occasion, leadership was shared between two or three individuals, but the implicit hierarchy remained.

I recognized the power of collective leadership as a graduate student. While my courses and lab work unsurprisingly followed the traditional model, I was fortunate to participate in a collaboration with a group of four other graduate students. What started organically as a discussion about how we wanted to share our research with the broader community grew into weekly meetings to plan the first independently organized Technology, Entertainment and Design (TEDx) conference at our campus.

Integrating Civic Engagement into General Education 147

I aspire to this type of collaborative, team-working space. This is why I was inspired by the collective spirit of the project we share in this chapter and believe that this leadership model served as a conduit for bringing together the strengths of the various members of our team. While I have some experience working in collaborative projects, this is the first time that I've really felt a sense of equity among all participants. Each individual was given room to learn from each other and apply their strengths where needed.

I plan to use a similar approach with my other projects, including the HIPs professional development program, so that faculty participants have a clearer contribution toward their own growth and the development of the program itself. Additionally, I plan to approach my scientific collaborations with this model and fully expect the research process to benefit as a whole.

Xuefei: In the information-intensive, digitized workplaces today, organizations have changed the way to organize work and manage teams. As more work is accomplished by cross-functional and interdisciplinary teams, organizations have increasingly applied a collective leadership model in their management practices. My understanding of this collective leadership is based on the premises of team-based decision making and cocreation of solutions and innovations. There are many factors contributing to the success of a collective leadership initiative. Based on my own involvement and experiences, I believe investing in team success and team trust building are two success factors.

I first became appreciative of the impact of collective leadership from my research collaboration with two senior scholars in my field (information systems) when I was a junior faculty. At that time, we became intrigued by the emerging phenomenon of crowdsourcing enabled by pervasive digital technologies and started to invest our time in uncovering the motivations of individuals from all walks of life to participate in taking micro-tasks in an online, boundaryless labor market. Crowdsourcing is an open-source work form, enabled and mediated by the internet and social media. It is the practice of obtaining needed services and content by soliciting voluntary contributions in the form of an open call from a large network of individuals rather than from an organization's employees or suppliers.[5] We aim to enhance our understanding of those crowd workers' experience and make recommendations for improving platform design and governance by the platform company, Amazon. Each of us took leadership in one part of the research project and contributed to the success of the project. We made decisions as a team and trusted each other's expertise. This collective leadership approach has led to the success of the project. Our research revealed an important message: although crowd workers benefit from the work flexibility and autonomy afforded by the digital platforms, they are exploited and marginalized from unfair, minimal pay and lack of accountability by job requesters. Our research work was published in *Management Information Systems (MIS) Quarterly*,[6] a top-tier information systems journal included in the *Financial Times* fifty journals (top journals in business and management disciplines), and was presented to the London School of Economics (LSE) Business Review's five-thousand-member blogging community.

While this academic collaboration was a success, it remained confined within the specific field of information systems. This is in direct contrast to the current project on community engagement, where representatives from different fields inside and outside of academia came together to guide the direction of this work. Indeed, the participants in this collaboration were, in part, the subjects of the research, which is very uncommon in academic work. To use the example from above, imagine if the crowdsourcing project was led in collaboration with not only the academics but also the crowd workers themselves, as well as the job requesters and company management. This is not something you see in academic collaborations. However, in this project it worked very well. The collective leadership was demonstrated from the start: we have developed not only a shared understanding about the project of community engagement and the minor but also a trust and bond among us. From all the team discussions and sharing of documents, I do feel that everyone in the group has made their best effort to bring their expertise to the process. For example, toward the end of spring 2020, we created the three different surveys mentioned earlier, amid the outbreaks of COVID-19 and under a tight schedule.

Specifically, everyone participated in the survey design and preview by offering feedback, and Philip worked hard on short notice to get approval from our institutional review board for research with human participants. At the beginning of spring 2020, when six of us faculty plus the community members and students met and laid out the project plan to the new stakeholders that had just joined us, we didn't know each other very well. At the end of the spring term in 2020, we had built a bond between us, placing trust in each other. During the process, we created a shared collaborative space that allowed us to trust in each other and understand our unique contributions to the work.

Gabbie: When I began my role at United Parents and Students, I was fortunate to have mentors and teammates who modeled collective leadership and taught me how to implement it throughout my organizing work. I learned to hold one-on-one meetings with parents and students, opening dialogue around community issues to listen openly to the perspectives held by community members. I practiced facilitating group meetings with an eye toward ensuring that everyone present had a chance to share their experiences and speak from their truth while working toward a common goal. I learned how to extend opportunities for research or action to those interested in gaining new skills or knowledge while avoiding assigning tasks hierarchically. Now, I strive to use principles of collective leadership throughout all my work, to promote collaborative action where all involved are engaged in the work and their unique contributions and skills valued.

The collective approach this group took in designing the community engagement minor during discussions with partners outside of the CSUDH community resonated with my own work in unexpected but pleasantly surprising ways. In particular, as a community partner and a member of the group who was initially unfamiliar with CSUDH and its institutional process for creating a minor, I expected to primarily listen and learn during the first few meetings I attended. I hoped to provide some peripheral input after I better understood how faculty members envisioned community engagement at CSUDH and their plan for creating a minor. Instead, I was asked directly about my opinions and ideas at the first meeting I attended. While I was pleasantly surprised to be welcomed into the group and invited to share, I still worried that my ideas might have been previously considered or discussed and would be superfluous, thus wasting valuable time. As I continued working with this group, however, I realized that while creating a community engagement minor was certainly the overarching goal, the process by which we were creating it was equally important. The group's encouragement to participate was not a superficial invitation but was rather demonstrative of an ontology that values the full participation of each group member, even if their participation comes at the expense of what we typically term "productivity": getting the most done in the shortest amount of time. This type of collaboration enabled everyone in the group to fully share their perspective and learn from each other's unique experiences.

The opportunity to watch and participate in a collaborative approach reminded me why my coworkers and I place such value on working within the collective leadership model. By operating in this way, the group was able to keep participants engaged and eager to share their perspective and thoughts without fear of judgment, thereby getting the best and most creative solutions we collectively had to offer while creating a sense of community and shared ownership. In my own role as a community engagement coordinator, the goals are similar: together identify issues, build solutions, and work within a mutual partnership. Collective leadership achieves each of these goals in an elegant and simple manner.

Culture Change

Institutions of higher education embody a shared set of policies, practices, and beliefs that affect the careers and lives of students, faculty, staff, and administrators. While each campus is unique in many ways, the institutional culture at CSUDH borrows from these common systems that impact how we communicate and accomplish goals. As each of us describe below, this project was enabled through an understanding of current institutional culture and our efforts to change these practices to succeed at our task.

Philip: The importance of culture change became clearer to me throughout my participation in this project. In my experience, higher education runs on models of success that are clearly outdated, based on individual accomplishments and encouraging the "siloization" of colleges and programs within the university, departments within the colleges, faculty within the departments, and ultimately students within classrooms. While universities are situated within communities, the walls of the ivory tower isolate academics from their surroundings. Even at CSUDH, whose history is rooted in the underserved communities of South-Central LA in the wake of the Watts Rebellion,[7] we struggle to break with the centuries-old habits of the academy. While outdated, this system continues to chug along until it is challenged.

The year 2020 provided ample challenges to test the stability of academia. The COVID-19 pandemic converged with the murder of George Floyd, and in the absence of leadership from elected politicians, the people sought guidance from their communities. This challenge was met by academic institutions in a variety of ways, and at CSUDH, classrooms were closed and anti-racist statements of solidarity were sent out. The moment was ripe for culture change. The community was calling out for change as protests engulfed neighborhoods in Los Angeles and across the world. How can we, as educators, researchers, and community organizers, answer that call?

Xuefei: To me, culture change at an institution starts by acknowledging that an institution's action plans are subject to change and ensuring that every stakeholder's voice is heard when making team decisions. While the overall purpose of this project was clear from the beginning, the specific and ultimate goals evolved through our meetings, reflections, and discovery, leading to more concrete actionable items and goals than planned. This was the result of a process that considered the voices of all participants. To me, one of the most memorable events is the meeting in November 2019 with all stakeholders mentioned earlier and the knowledge cocreation by the multiple stakeholders attending the meeting. Numerous questions emerged during the project meetings, including: How is community engagement or service learning (SL) defined? How is community engagement perceived by different stakeholders (i.e., students, faculty, community partners, university administrators)? What course activities are considered community engagement? What skills and knowledge are considered essential for students engaging in CE projects in their courses? Would a CE minor appeal to students and community partners?

I was very impressed by several observations. One is the voice of several community partners: the attendees not only expressed their support for students and for the university's initiative in enhancing student learning from community engagement but also offered helpful guidelines in building a long-term relationship between the community and the university. One common theme from the community partners' voice was the efforts required of community partners in hosting and mentoring students in the community organizations. The other important voice is the voice of students. A group of students from an anthropology course taught by Sarah Taylor (one of the FLC participants, and a coauthor of chapter 6 in this book, where this student research was also mentioned) attended the meeting and shared their class project outcomes. As part of their course requirements, those students completed a research project with CSUDH students, faculty, and staff about their experiences, views, and opinions surrounding the creation of a civic engagement minor. Their findings revealed that overall, reactions to a CE minor are positive, but more details about a potential CE minor were needed. In addition to the anthropology class students, two social work students and an arts student also attended the meeting and shared their viewpoints about community engagement activities.

This multi-stakeholder meeting made me realize the importance of bringing multiple perspectives to efforts to create the minor, and it made me appreciate more about the purpose of promoting community engagement among our students. I appreciated the data-driven, multifaceted approach this group has taken in the discovering CE/SL efforts and in the development of a community engagement minor.

Gabbie: As mentioned earlier, in my work at United Parents and Students, we strive to ensure that all voices are heard and valued in our decisions and work to institutionalize practices that reflect those values. We hold one-on-one conversations with individuals to find out more about their perspectives and self-interests and host open-door meetings wherein all opinions and ideas are welcome and encouraged. However, as a nonprofit organization, we still rely on outside funders and grants to sustain our staff and operations. Most funders are primarily drawn to applicants who can demonstrate a history of results and measurable impacts. Sometimes, our need to attain funding overshadows the importance of the process of our work, which can sometimes feel slow or difficult to explain to a third party who might be unfamiliar with collective leadership. There is sometimes a tension between our need to produce results and the practices that guide our work.

Despite this tension, working within a model of collective leadership is paramount to the success of our larger organizational mission of shifting power to those who have historically been denied it. United Parents and Students primarily works in areas of Los Angeles that have not only suffered from historic disinvestment from governmental and nongovernmental institutions but whose residents have also, throughout history and currently, been intentionally prohibited from accessing avenues to wealth and institutional power through policies, laws, and practices. However, United Parents and Students was founded on the idea that every individual has an innate and inherent power to shape the world around them. We strive to help everyone, but especially those who have been historically silenced, who recognize their own intrinsic power and use it to advocate for the world they want to see. Large-scale social justice and equity will of course require policy changes, reinvestment, and social reckoning. Our hope is that by building a foundation for change on the understanding that we all have ideas, skills, and input that are needed and wanted, we might begin to build together the world as it should be, even if only in our small corner of it.

We have described above our experiences using collective leadership and research in action to implement a community engagement minor on our campus. By bringing together multiple voices from various stakeholders, including faculty, administrators, students, and local community partners, we individually felt empowered to contribute to the overall goals of the project. This strengthened our collaborative work by leveraging our individual expertise and gave us insight into the various challenges that exist in this type of work. Additionally, the bonds of trust that developed between the participants permitted us to explore areas of interest outside of our siloed careers. Together, this experience brought new insights into not only how to accomplish the specific tasks of the project but also how our ongoing work within our organizations can be done differently, changing the culture of work one project at a time.

Reflections on Writing during Uncertain Times

In the same vein of our work together on the community engagement project, this chapter was written from a collaborative lens. Though the chapter lead (Philip) handled logistics, much of the writing was done with input from all three authors. Our starting point was a discussion about our experience over the past year and how our individual backgrounds informed those experiences. We then created a loose structure to share our perspectives as individual participants in this work. We concluded by reflecting on the entire experience of collaborative writing and how we see this work applying to our future aspirations.

Writing this chapter during 2020–21 was impacted by the ongoing pandemic and sociopolitical unrest that took place during this time. The protests led by Black Lives Matter and the fight against systemic racism evidenced in continuous policing practices became overshadowed by an exhausting election season that bled into a national coup attempt and the escalation of white supremacist violence on January 6, 2021. Simultaneously, the COVID-19 pandemic has ravaged our communities, especially in Los Angeles County. These realities directly impacted the work we do, whether as educators trying to navigate remote teaching with students who have unstable internet access, trying to learn in home environments that feel the stress of unemployment, stay-at-home orders, overburdened health care systems, and the risks of continuing essential work to make ends meet, or as a community organizer working with families that are out of work, worried about rent and housing stability, unable to afford groceries, and facing disproportionate rates of infection and death.

All the while we recognize and are proud of the work of community organizers and service organizations, health care workers, frontline employees, and all those who have taken care of their communities during these trying times, which makes it difficult to acknowledge our personal hardships in a year that has been devastating, emotionally taxing, and downright exhausting. Each of our communities has been heavily impacted by these factors as we have had to face the realities of economic hardships, social isolation, racism, and death of friends, neighbors, and family. Each day felt heavier than the last, making it particularly difficult to revisit our work from the past year in the midst of so much chaos. Along with much of the country, we felt physically and emotionally drained.

Writing this chapter has been a challenging experience, but ultimately a rewarding and fulfilling one. This style of writing was new to all of us. Rather than considering our accomplishments through an academic or professional lens, we were all challenged to reflect on our personal experiences in our shared work, and how our experience of collective leadership influenced our lives, both professionally and personally. We then were challenged to write about those reflections in a style that felt personal and intimate rather than objective and scientific, as most of us are accustomed to. Writing in this way requires more emotional space than traditional academic or professional writing, which felt in short supply in 2020. However, we also recognized the urgency of writing this chapter now as an example of how to bring together diverse perspectives to accomplish a common goal. The model of collective leadership we created made it possible for ideas to emerge that may otherwise not have been seen or heard. This in turn made it less intimidating to approach writing the chapter. While we each have different levels of education and experience in writing, the collective model allowed us to feel safe with sharing our personal thoughts and experiences. By deeply valuing and eliciting the contributions of each member of the team, collective leadership opens up vast creative potential that might have otherwise been missed.

As we look to the future, it seems clear that collective leadership has a role to play, though the specifics are less certain. At the university, there are some applications that stand out. Whether in the classroom or the research lab, students should be seen as equal stakeholders in their education/training. Giving voice to students will not only provide motivation for them to actively participate but also allow them to shape the experience based on their own interests, backgrounds, and future goals. Beyond students, how we engage with our faculty and administrative colleagues can also benefit from this approach. We look forward to building a community at the university that uses collective leadership to forge partnerships across disparate groups.

However, we also recognize the challenges that come with this approach. It will require each individual to first understand their personal goals and how they align with the objectives of the whole team. Care must be exercised in these group settings so that each member feels safe to speak openly about their perspectives, shaped by their experiences and guided by their aspirations. We also recognize that this type of work can be more demanding of mental energy, with frequent reflections on your personal background and opening up to a group of colleagues. Ultimately, if this can be achieved, the individuals will find the experience rewarding as they explore how their colleagues' personal and professional interests connect with their own.

In very uncertain times, it is not clear what might come when collective leadership is applied in various settings. What would emerge if a local governing body were to apply principles of collective leadership to their work? Whose voices would come to the forefront if given the opportunity? What would those individuals say if someone were to take the time to listen? What would the world look like if we valued and took seriously the contributions of every individual?

The answers to these questions are unknown, which in turn creates possibility. In a world where hope feels uncertain and distant, having a method that creates multitudes of possibilities feels energizing and necessary. At a time when violent ideologies of superiority have been given authority and positions of power, it is essential that we look toward new ways of working together that encourage participation and honor the experience and wisdom of each individual.

Notes

1. Throughout this chapter, we will use the terms "civic engagement," "community engagement," "service learning," and "internships" interchangeably to refer to those practices that connect academic education/scholarship with community projects.

2. More information about this project can be found at Bringing Theory to Practice (BT2P), Projects of the BT2P Community, "Creating a Crucible Moment: Building an Integrative Civic Engagement Pathway between California's Post-Secondary Systems," https://bttop.org/bt2p_projects/creating-a-crucible-moment-building-an-integrative-civic-engagement-pathway-between-californias-post-secondary-systems/ (accessed March 2, 2022).

3. High-impact educational practices (HIPs) are a collection of pedagogical strategies shown to increase student retention and academic success. They include community service learning, intensive writing courses, collaborative assignments/projects, diversity/global learning, common intellectual experiences, learning communities, first-year seminars/experiences, and research. See George Kuh, Ken O'Donnell, and Carol Geary Schneider, "HIPs at Ten," *Change: The Magazine of Higher Learning* 49, no. 5 (2017): 8–16.

4. For more information about United Parents and Students, visit https://unitedparentsandstudents.org/ (accessed March 2, 2022).
5. Jeff Howe, "The Rise of Crowdsourcing," *Wired*, June 1, 2006, 1–4.
6. Xuefei (Nancy) Deng, K. D. Joshi, and Robert D. Galliers, "The Duality of Empowerment and Marginalization in Microtask Crowdsourcing: Giving Voice to the Less Powerful through Value Sensitive Design," *MIS Quarterly* 42, no. 2 (2016): 279–302.
7. The institution first opened its doors in 1965 in affluent Palos Verdes. It was relocated per order of the California governor, as an economic development strategy, following the 1965 Watts Rebellion. See CSUDH, "50th Anniversary Watts Rebellion Commemoration," https://www.csudh.edu/watts/ (accessed March 2, 2022).

Conclusion

DISCOVERIES AND REVELATIONS, DREAMING OF POSSIBILITIES

Maria Avila

> Our tradition asserts that transformation is not only possible but also absolutely necessary for continued survival of all people and the planet.... Our work today is about redefining humanity and transforming our relationships with each other and with the land.
> —*Charlene A. Carruthers*

Being aware of our stories and sharing them with others is one way to awaken us to the richness of our traditions, and to their teachings about our struggles, victories, and possibilities for a better world. For Charlene Carruthers this can also fuel hope and imagination.[1] For me, this is central to building collective leadership. This is how we learn together about what actions we are ready to take as a collective. We do this in relationship with each other, as we begin to realize our roles in the future of our institutions, organizations, and communities. As mentioned in chapter 1, when I decided to write this book in a reflective, collaborative format, my motivation stemmed from my interest in learning about what took place in the five projects in this book, from the participants' perspective, but also an interest in continuing building collective leadership through the writing of the book. While we explored several themes during our reflective conversations and writing, two questions lingered in my mind throughout the projects, after the projects, and throughout the collaborative writing process:

1. Was my organizing successful in building collective leadership?
2. Did the projects create culture change in and outside academia?

Part of this is driven by an aspiration, a strong desire even, to jump to a beautiful and ideal conclusion. Yes, definitely, of course my organizing to build collective leadership was successful, and culture change occurred in all projects! As if all that was needed was to write about this so that others could follow my example, and for all of us to celebrate my wonderful and innovative achievement. It could no doubt become part of "best practices" of some kind. I think of this as my prophetic voice, which has little room for doubt, or reflexivity, to use academic language. This may also be called aspirational (in academia), or wishful thinking, which we all experience from time to time. I have experienced it many times as an organizer inside and outside of academia.

But in my current role and training as an academic, I must interrogate, be reflexive (or . . . doubtful?) about whether and how my organizing in the five projects really built collective leadership to create culture change. This reflexivity also includes acknowledging that even if I succeeded wholly or partially, I also encountered challenges along the way. So let me be reflexive, as I share what I learned about the projects' effect in my organizing efforts.

Organizing to Build Collective Leadership

While the projects were happening, I had many moments in which I saw signs that creating a collaborative space to think, learn, cocreate, and share stories together would eventually lead to enhancing the leadership skills of participants in each project, and that their (until then) individual civic agency would transform into collective civic agency. This is what I mean by building collective leadership. I further saw how this led to shaping and achieving the specific, evolving goals of each project. This is what I mean by taking action together. This is all part of my organizing approach. But I was not sure at the time, I have to say, if participants were fully aware of this process. And so, one way to check in with them about this was to have them write quotes illustrating what they learned and what they experienced, which I inserted in the final reports for each project. While I can see how I was creating a somewhat collaborative writing process, I now wonder if my main motivation was driven by wanting them to give me proof that my organizing had worked, so that we could relay this to whoever had sponsored the projects (i.e., funders and potential funders in and outside of academia).

In hindsight, I can now say that in most projects, participants were not fully aware of my organizing purpose and methodology for creating a space where they could grow as leaders, individually and collectively, and where they could patiently allow themselves to be part of shaping the projects' purposes and objectives, so that they would achieve the objectives together. And except for my last project, I did not feel clear enough of my combined methodologies of research in action and narrative inquiry well enough to explain them in detail. I remember also experiencing a feeling of not wanting to offend them by stating that they needed or could grow as leaders, and that I firmly believe that we can best achieve culture change by enacting our collective leadership. This has been a revelation to me, shaping up from one project to the next, and becoming even more clear as I reflect about it now.

I don't think I ever experienced this type of doubt during my IAF organizing. Not that I did not experience doubt at all back then. Anyone who has been an organizer can attest to plenty of doubtful moments in the process of organizing. But not the type of doubts I now realize I experienced with the projects. The difference might be that my role as an IAF organizer was explicit to everyone. I did not need to look for language and methodologies appropriate to them as an audience. Aha, this means that through the projects, I have been growing as an organizer with a different audience and in a different context! I am now a civically engaged academic using this platform to continue my organizing with faculty and other professional colleagues, but still in my IAF organizing interest of enhancing democracy. I am coconstructing this identity for myself in the collaborative spaces I am creating, in a relational and hopefully more humane way than what the competitive and siloed academic culture tends to allow. This discovery is very valuable to me. This is about my changing place of knowing and who I am becoming. The lessons learned through the chapters about my colleagues' post-project reflections are valuable too. They illustrate their own thinking processes related to what I was attempting to do as an organizer. I will use their first or informal names throughout this reflection, as I did in the opening section of each chapter, because I feel more connected to them in this way than if I use their formal names.

Kathy and Enrique (chapter 3), for instance, comment in their chapter that they were new to the research methodologies of participatory research and narrative inquiry. This at first, they write, conflicted with their research training, which is "heavily based on the use of empirical and quantitative evidence." Enrique shares a powerful lesson he learned about narrative inquiry while reflecting and writing with Kathy: "As many others did, I treated my professional activities as separate from my personal life; I would go so far as to say that I actively kept them separate in order to protect and foster each of these spaces independently.... What I had not considered up to this point was that both of these sides of myself were connected to a singular story and that, as such, my story could be used to better understand choices and commitments to my work and my home life alike." He speaks of the powerful moment when he realized that his personal story could help him make sense of his family and professional life, thereby helping "build the purposeful career I was looking to establish."

Similarly, Kathy reflects on how her narrative and how her perspective about her race and gender changed through the antiracist demonstrations the summer of 2020. She writes that while she has evolved in her views throughout the years, "even leaving one rigid Christian denomination for a more liberal one. I always saw myself as sensitive to diversity as I was married to a Korean gentleman and we raised our children together." Yet she writes that prior to the summer of 2020 she had not realized that she "was brought up in a very narrow, white, conservative environment." She adds: "I have to say, 2020 was the first time I said to myself, 'Why have I let all these white men dictate what I'm thinking?'"

While Kathy and Enrique have become clear about my research methodologies through their collaborative reflecting and writing, Aixle and Ray (chapter 4) were introduced to community organizing and narrative inquiry from the beginning of my project with them. After all, I was asked to do this project by Ref Rodriguez, a colleague with whom I collaborated during my time at Occidental's Center for Community Based Learning (CCBL). Back then, Ref was part of a regional organizing project with schools surrounding Occidental that aimed to create a college-going culture in that region. At the time of this project (2016–17) he was a Los Angeles school board member. Because he was familiar with my community organizing approach, he asked me to create an organizing culture with his staff. It stands to reason, therefore, that this chapter almost gives a primer on specific community-organizing practices as they describe their experience and what was achieved.

Aixle and Ray's familiarity with my narrative inquiry approach is clear in the framing of the chapter with their narratives. For as long as I have known Ray, he has always been comfortable and clear about the role that his narrative plays in his work. His story as a descendent from immigrant grandparents from Chinese and Nicaraguan origins and the way in which this connected with his work at Board District 5 is powerful. As he reflects on his role in this job while working in Northeast Los Angeles communities, he writes that he was aware that he was in fact working for and with the communities that had raised him. Reading this makes me wonder: How often does anyone have the opportunity to do this through our jobs? And how many of us would think about it with this level of clarity? This is strikingly rare, in my view. Aixle, on the other hand, has always seemed more comfortable talking specifics about work-related things such as purpose, objectives, methodologies, and time lines. Through this collaborative reflecting and writing process, however, she was able to find parts of her narrative that connect with her professional interests. As she shares, her values of service to those more marginalized stem from her roots as a Catholic daughter of parents who emigrated from the Philippines. As she elaborates, it is also clear to me that this is where her leadership skills come from: "From high school to college, I became actively involved in Christian leadership groups that helped organize activities for other students. Together, we planned engaging masses to which our peers could feel more connected (e.g., utilizing props, modern dance, and popular music)."

In my assessment, all participants evolved as a collective of leaders who worked together toward specific goals. Perhaps the authors of chapter 5 more specifically mention this. George, for instance, shares that through his experience as part of the collective of leaders in the Imagining America Southern California cluster, he learned how to build a collaborative partnership with a community artist and with his undergraduate and graduate students in the founding of a history museum in Boyle Heights. George would often share with the cluster about this project while it was evolving. I remember going to the opening ceremony of the first exhibit at the museum, which included a play. What I remember most is when George shared the stage with his community artist partner and with his students. George introduced them, and then each one of them shared stories about their respective roles in this project.

In this same chapter, Alan, Celestina, George, and Rissi summarize their views about why collective leadership is effective in the cluster, in this way: "Hierarchies tend to magnify the faults of those at the top and stifle the contributions of those at the bottom. With horizontal collective leadership we are free to teach and learn from each other according to our abilities and our needs. This keeps the cluster vital by helping us move forward individually, which in turn makes it possible to move forward collectively in response to internal initiatives or changing circumstances." The authors credit this type of leadership and the relational work of the cluster prior to the pandemic for the smooth transition to virtual meetings in the fall of 2020. In fact, Alan and other members joined the cluster during our first virtual meeting. The long-term relationships Alan had with some of us in the cluster led to his role in the core leadership within the same semester.

The horizontal, collective leadership practiced in the cluster also made it possible to transition from Celestina to Rissi as lead organizers during the summer of 2020. With the sudden changes in demands on all of us midway through the spring of 2020, we stopped meetings as a cluster. During the summer, Celestina, Rissi, and I were able to meet and strategize about ways to resume cluster meetings. We did not know if others would want to meet virtually, but as we began to meet in the fall, we found out that others were wanting to reconnect and reflect together about what we were all experiencing through the pandemic, the anti-racist movement, and the presidential election. Folks also shared the ways in which they were learning how to continue their community engagement projects virtually. While virtual spaces will never replace the camaraderie, the eating and talking before and after meetings, catching up personally and professionally, and all that can happen through in-person meetings, we, humans that we are, will always find ways to adjust and pivot. And so, we in the cluster did.

As our campuses and organizations have gradually resumed in-person work and classes, it has become apparent that not everyone is ready to leave the virtual modality behind. Some prefer to remain fully virtual, while others are leaning toward hybrid modalities by combining virtual and in-person activities. In the cluster, all large meetings have remained virtual, while some core leadership and one-on-one meetings have been in person. This is not ideal for the relational organizing approach I use. I have found the virtual platform to be very limiting and had hoped that at some point during the spring semester we would resume meetings in person. To my disappointment, however, most cluster participants do not share my interest. As of June 2022, the continued increase in numbers of cases of COVID-19 and the spread of new variants in several regions of the country make going fully back in person even less likely. These are uncertain times, for sure, and it may be that the best modality for a while may be virtual or hybrid. This is clearly a source of tension for me.

Here, I use the opportunity to reflect about other tensions I have felt for a few years as the cluster's founder and organizer. I created this cluster with the clear intention to use community-organizing practices to create culture change in higher education and the surrounding communities. While I was hoping that the specific parts of the culture that required change would emerge from those attending cluster meetings, a specific part of the culture I proposed was around civically engaged scholarship to be recognized, valued, and rewarded. The small group of colleagues with whom I began the conversations about the cluster had been part of my organizing work for a while, and therefore they were aware that I would be using community-organizing practices in this project. Their own interests in creating change in the cultures of their institutions evolved through many conversations, and through sharing stories of specific engagement projects we were involved in on our campuses and communities. I remember, for instance, that George's stories were usually about access and equity for students of color, particularly those of immigrant origin. Celestina's stories were often related to Native American Indigenous people.

While we in the core leadership group were always solidifying the purpose of the cluster through our respective projects, this was not the case with others who joined as the cluster evolved. This has been a significant source of tension for me, but also a source of significant learning and growth (no pain, no gain?). My vision from the beginning was that we would ask cluster members to host the meetings, and they would use this as an opportunity to introduce their colleagues, students, and community partners to the cluster. This was the intent in rotating meetings across campuses. Those in the core leadership of the cluster and I would then be sharing our thoughts about the purpose of the cluster, and others would join in conversation about it. After two or three years of trying this, we realized that attendance at the cluster meetings was not consistent from those outside of the core leadership, and therefore repeating ourselves about the purpose of the cluster and about role in Imagining America as a national organization was not interesting enough for others. Eventually, we realized that for most, the cluster serves as a place to learn about each other's engagement projects and have conversations not common in other spaces in our institutions and organizations. This is great, in and of itself, but I am not sure it will lead to creating culture change on their campuses and communities. The four authors of chapter 5 are part of the core leadership, and except for Alan, they joined the cluster at the beginning or within the first year. The collaborative reflecting and writing process of this book has brought us to reassess the purpose of the cluster. Are we OK if the cluster does not lead to creating culture change for folks other than those in the core leadership? If not, what should the purpose be? Am I OK with this?

These are questions we in the core leadership reflected about as we moved into 2021–22 and as I retook my role as lead organizer of the cluster in the fall of 2021. From these reflections emerged the idea to experiment with a research in action project focused on teaching and learning about community organizing to create culture change on our campuses and organizations, during the spring of 2022. We saw this as an opportunity to explore whether my original interest in creating the cluster would be of interest to others outside the core leadership. We explicitly shared this purpose with those who had been attending cluster meetings for several years and with others that have joined recently. We asked if they could commit to attending five meetings between February and June. Many responded that they were not able to make this commitment and asked us to reconnect with them at the end of this project to find out what we had learned. At the end, between eight and twelve people engaged in the five meetings, which were all virtual. The core leadership will be meeting later in the summer to reflect about what we learned, and how this can inform the purpose, format, and meeting modality for next year.

While participants in all five projects mention narrative inquiry in some way, Joanna and Sarah (chapter 6) refer to narrative as their funds of knowledge and explain that this concept "recognizes the importance of lived experience through family, household, and community interactions that learners bring to their formal education."[2] They then expand on their narratives through the concept of positionality. Joanna positions herself as the daughter of Guatemalan immigrants. Her parents' experiences of struggle and their words of wisdom are ingrained in Joanna's mind, and this inspiration is why she decided to become a sociologist. She writes: "To this day, my mother's words of wisdom are what keeps me grounded: '*échale ganas al estudio porque la educación es muy valioso, algo que nadie te puede quitar*' (keep up with your studies because education is really valuable, it is something that no one can take away from you)."

Unlike Joanna's clarity about the connection between her narrative and her work, Sarah writes that finding this connection was a struggle for her throughout this project. Her life as an academic in the United States is very different from her research with Indigenous farmers in a small village in Yucatán, Mexico. Only after reflecting and writing with Joanna was she able to find such a connection, by thinking about things she learned and was encouraged to do while growing up, but also about the commonalities between these two worlds: "What they share are the mundane moments that make up a life, like conversations over meals, interactions with neighbors, and family dynamics. I think that a lot of the connection between my personal narrative and my research is just recognizing the role of culture in our lives and what a human experience all of this is, as opposed to being an American experience, or a white experience, or a Maya experience, or a Mexican experience. It's just this very human condition, so that's the connection I see."

Joanna and Sarah discuss in great detail how they experienced, perhaps for the first time in their careers, the collaborative process in the project I did with them (and with other colleagues in this project). They remember that the meetings usually started by checking in with each other about life and about progress with their curriculum work. In their words:

> Through our check-ins, we began to share more about our lives within and outside of academia. We engaged in deep discussions about how we define, interpret, and apply community engagement in our scholarship, teaching, and service. And as we discussed our respective projects, we provided each other feedback and support. Hence, through a series of conversations, reflection activities, and writing sessions, we developed a sense of community and began to reimagine what was possible in the classroom, in our respective departments, and across our campus. In the process, we built on each other's strengths and began to connect on a deeper level. To this day, many of us continue to stay connected, not because we happen to work at the same institution but because we genuinely care for each other and desire to replicate our experience across campus.

Philip, Nancy (Xuefei), and Gabbie (chapter 7) write their reflections about the ways in which the collaborative space in which they participated, and the combined research methodology I used led to the creation of a community engagement minor focused primarily on CSUDH's general education curriculum. Philip, for instance, describes how collaborative inquiry evolved in the project, which started with an assessment of existing community engagement teaching on the campus, after which "we embarked on a process of inquiry about what we know and what we would like to know." This process led the group to eventually design two surveys for faculty and one for community partners.

After a few meetings, participants in this project came to realize that I was using community-organizing practices in creating this type of collaborative inquiry process, but they did not always know how I operationalized this. For example, I knew Nancy was interested in surveys and data analysis from a presentation she did for the Academic Senate a few years back, while I was chair of the Senate's Faculty Policy Committee. With this knowledge, I asked her if she would be willing and interested in analyzing the data from SLICE's past surveys and then sharing the findings with the group. Nancy agreed to do this, which set the tone for her specific role throughout the project with the new surveys we collectively developed.

I noticed this topic drew Philip's attention, judging from his more active participation in the group's conversations. I asked if he would like to help Nancy; he agreed and joined Nancy as they led the group's collaborative design and analysis of the surveys. Our group's decision to assess existing community engagement teaching on the campus also naturally provided a space for members of the Center for Service-Learning, Internships, and Civic Engagement (SLICE), and Nancy's role involved working closely with them.

The survey for community partners created a space for Gabbie to play a specific role. This was especially helpful in Gabbie's engagement in the project, as she developed the confidence to participate in a group of mostly academics. This is how she reflects about what she thought her role would be in the project, and how it evolved: "I hoped to provide some peripheral input after I better understood how faculty members envisioned community engagement at CSUDH and their plan for creating a minor. Instead, I was asked directly about my opinions and ideas at the first meeting I attended. While I was pleasantly surprised to be welcomed into the group and invited to share, I still worried that my ideas might have been previously considered or discussed and would be superfluous, thus wasting valuable time." Gabbie was key in coming up with questions we ended up including in this survey, identifying community partners we could reach out to, and interpreting the findings.

Being able to intentionally involve different community engagement stakeholders is something I had never been able to do before to the extent to which it took place in this project. I have explored this type of multi-stakeholder participation pretty much in all my work as a practitioner and as a scholar because I believe that collective leadership across diversity of all kinds can be more effective in creating culture change, and including different stakeholders' voices is also part of enhancing democratic participation. Prior to this project, I was able to do this, but not at the level of equal partnership in this project. I learned from previous experiences that mixing stakeholders did not seem to resonate at all for some, or only slightly for others. This time, I brought up the idea gradually and slowly, in conversation early in the first semester.

Once all were open to including other stakeholders, I proposed taking our idea of creating the minor to a meeting where we would invite students, community partners, and representatives from SLICE and the Office of External Relations. This was the first opportunity for some of my colleagues to be in conversation with different stakeholders in this collaborative, cocreative learning process. I debriefed and reflected with the group of faculty about being in the learning process with multi-stakeholders in our following meeting, and their enthusiasm about what they had experienced led me to propose that we invite some of those who attended that meeting to our group the following semester. For the following three semesters of the project, our group was a mix of all stakeholders who had attended this meeting, thus significantly enriching the process of building collective leadership by contributing different perspectives to what we ended up accomplishing. It was this multi-stakeholder group that was able to collaboratively create the minor. In addition to this main goal of the project, we were able to create a faculty liaison to work with SLICE, with financial support from SLICE and the Office of Undergraduate Studies. We were also able to share what we did, as well as the methodology used with the campus community and with community partners at SLICE's annual symposium in the spring of 2021, the last semester of this project.

Reading what my colleagues wrote about their experience as part of a collective of leaders is evidence that my methodology worked, even if not in the same way for all projects. It is also clear to me that the reflective, collaborative writing process of this book project has given us the space to reflect on our work together, retrospectively, and it has also strengthened our relationships with each other. I now share my reflections on the ways in which we created culture change, at what level, and to what end.

Creating Culture Change

Circling back to what I wrote in chapter 1, I organize because I believe our democracy is fragmented, which affects all sectors of society, including higher education. Through organizing, I aim to create spaces where we can learn how to act and be collaborative, reflective, and deliberative, and how to take action together.

Without such spaces, the culture dominating our institutions and organizations is one of hyperactivity; the more we produce, the more successful we are supposed to be. There is a general perception that more is better. In higher education, we often refer to silos when speaking of the ways in which faculty do our teaching and research. Faculty often talk about feeling overwhelmed with scholarship and service responsibilities, and about not feeling supported by the administration. From previous research and experience, I know that administrators often feel that faculty are difficult to engage with, and that they don't always comply with rules and guidelines imposed on administrators by external entities (i.e., government and other funders, CSU and other higher education systems). There is some truth to each side's arguments, but there are no natural spaces where all can have conversations about ways to be more understanding of and collaborative with each other. This lack of collaboration is true for most academic departments. The hyperactive and fragmented culture exists outside of academia too, including the not-for-profit civic sector, where most of our community partners work. Through my colleagues' chapters and my own reflections about the five projects, I can see that culture change occurred in all projects to various degrees, and yet we have so much work to do to create healthier conditions where we work and in our communities.

I find hope and evidence of culture change, for example, in the chapter written by Aixle and Ray. As mentioned, this project was created with the clear intention of teaching community organizing to Aixle and Ray, along with others in their office. The purpose of doing this to build civic capacity among their constituents, though not fully clear from the beginning, evolved through workshops, coaching in the field, and written reflections. At the end of our yearlong project, they had a general understanding of how to change their service-oriented approach with their constituents to one that aimed to build civic capacity through community organizing.

Through this post-reflection, I realize that they took it on themselves to continue learning together after our project ended, and this is how they found specific ways to teach organizing skills to their constituents. Aixle comments: "One of our biggest learnings was that everything is grounded on relationships and that our charge was not to empower our communities but to *activate* the power that they already possessed. The families and community members in [Board District] 5 possessed a wealth of knowledge and expertise of their own communities' needs and opportunities through their lived experiences. It was our job to help them see their experiences as valuable assets that can catalyze them to take action to improve the conditions in their own communities."

As I have reflected with Aixle and Ray, through our project together and their work after the project ended, the culture of their office was radically changed. Their passion about community organizing and the way in which it transformed the culture of their office is palpable throughout the chapter, and so are their reflections about their own transformation, personally and professionally. In the end, the whole staff succeeded in transitioning from individual to collective agency. I returned to work with their office on a short-term project a year later and had an opportunity to witness and experience their collective trust and the strong bonds they had with each other while exercising their collective agency. The entire staff left this office in 2019, when a new board member was elected, but they continue supporting each other in their respective new jobs and in their personal lives. I know this because I have continued collaborating with some of them in some way, including, for example, inviting them to speak to my classes.

This to me is an indication that it is in fact possible to create a collaborative culture outside of academia, but it requires a great deal of learning and intentionality.

While Aixle and Ray offer extensive details about community organizing and its role in creating culture change in their work with their constituents, Alan, Celestina, George, and Rissi discuss culture change in detail and give specific examples of what this means to them. Their clarity about culture change begins with their values: "The values of community, critical reflection, personal narrative, and collective leadership guide us in considering ways to shift the individualistic and competitive culture of academia toward one that inspires collective imagination, knowledge making, and civic action." They contrast the deliberate and slow process they use in the cluster with the more high-paced and productivity-focused culture that predominates in higher education.

Thus, Celestina illustrates with a story about an initiative to integrate community-based learning language that took over a decade of slow and intentional organizing through relationship building and strategizing with faculty and administration. I was still director of CCBL when we started this effort, and I remember that we took it up to the Faculty Council. But as Alan mentions, we had not done the necessary strategic and relational work, and so we did not succeed then. I also remember when this happened in 2016, years after I had left Occidental. Celestina shared this at a cluster meeting as an example of the type of culture change the cluster aims to see happen across member institutions.

Alan gives an example of a community-based learning class he created and taught when he was a full-time faculty member at Occidental. I remember this class, but especially the strategic and intentional process Alan used in building a collaborative with three other faculty colleagues at Occidental to team teach the class, and with teachers from a nearby community partner high school to create a community project that would help students pass Algebra 1 to increase their chances of graduating.

In response to the lack of community she experienced as a student at USC, Rissi shares that she began to gather students from different disciplines who were also seeking to be part of a community. Eventually, these efforts resulted in the collaborative creation of a community organization focused on community arts, which now (years after Rissi graduated) partners with universities, nonprofit and for-profit organizations, and government.

While these examples did not happen in the cluster, it seems to me that their reflections on the culture change while writing the chapter led them to add clarity to their own concept of culture change and the ways in which they have been part of such efforts in their institutions. Their examples help create conversation in cluster meetings, which is very useful especially because attendance at these meetings is not consistent, and culture change is not a concept that is common in organizing for social change. My hope is that these examples and their definition of culture change are also helpful to readers.

Alan, Celestina, George, and Rissi conclude that the events we are living through worldwide have only made the need for culture change more urgent. As they see it: "We need to dig deeply into what democratic process means in this context, beginning with a recognition that the American public includes communities that might not speak English. . . . We must also recognize that a substantial portion of the American public is more interested in hanging on to its privileges than in democracy. . . . The way we talk with each other, develop relationships, and foster a culture of mutual respect is a good way to think about change and how to do things differently."

In conversations with my colleagues, project participants, and now coauthors, they all conclude that through their participation in the five projects they were able to change parts of the culture of their institutions. I agree, and thus confirm what I sensed before checking in with them about whether my organizing led to creating culture change and to their growth as a collective of leaders. They also, through the collaborative writing process, have engaged their imagination about ways in which they can work toward changing other parts of their institutions and communities.

What is less clear to me is whether they will actually be able to take their energy and organizing skills as individuals and/or as collectives of leaders to other spaces where they can teach others how to do this, and thus grow this movement to create more collaborative, more humane cultures in places where we work and live. Doubting that this will take place has nothing to do with their desire and skills to do it. It has everything to do with comments I made earlier about why we need culture change in the first place. Some of my coauthors have made similar observations. I am referring here to what feels to me like a cult of hyperactivity and its symbolizing of success. Without developing an awareness that this is the context in which we work and live, it will be very challenging for us as a society to make the time to create spaces where we can learn how to get off this hyperactivity treadmill and begin to cocreate more humane ways of being.

Culture Change in Tumultuous Times

Creating culture change takes a different dimension in these times of COVID-19 and anti-racism. Reflecting about the impact of the pandemic, the anti-racist movement, and the events related to the presidential election in 2020, Joanna and Sarah share that they found themselves managing their students' anxieties and fears while dealing with the changes in their own lives. They add: "To this end, these unforeseen circumstances have impacted how we engage with each other in all areas of our lives, what and how we teach, how we continue our research virtually, and how we use our service commitments to continue to promote social change." The authors end with a call to use the unprecedented moment we are experiencing worldwide as an opportunity, perhaps a mandate, to interrogate and reimagine academia and its role in our democratic society. They conclude that prioritizing civically engaged scholarship is an important step to begin this process.

Philip, Nancy, and Gabbie found the collaborative format of their project very helpful and inspiring, and their reflections about using collective leadership to create culture change are particularly relevant to this historic moment. In this context, they write about the process of collaborative writing, including its challenges: "This style of writing was new to all of us. Rather than considering our accomplishments through an academic or professional lens, we were all challenged to reflect on our personal experiences in our shared work, and how our experience of collective leadership influenced our lives, both professionally and personally." They conclude that writing this way "requires more emotional space than traditional academic or professional writing, which felt in short supply in 2020." They add: "However, we also recognized the urgency of writing this chapter now as an example of how to bring together diverse perspectives to accomplish a common goal." They raise a set of questions as they ponder about what the world would look like if collective leadership were adopted: "What would emerge if a local governing body were to apply principles of collective leadership to their work? Whose voices would come to the forefront if given the opportunity? What would those individuals say if someone were to take the time to listen? What would the world look like if we valued and took seriously the contributions of every individual?" They assert that our not knowing the answers to these questions in fact creates possibility, and that collective leadership is essential especially to countering the existing culture of violence.

Final Thoughts

Reflecting about the five projects and the context in which I approached each of them helps me understand the extent to which we were able to act as a collective of leadership to create culture change. This also helps me understand how much the pandemic and the anti-racist movement may have influenced our retrospective reflections about these projects. It is evident to me that none of us were aware of the extent to which we were acting as a collective of leaders or were able to create culture change, with the level of clarity we now have, after our reflective conversations and collaborative writing. Through the process of writing this book, we have been able to further our learning about the research methodologies I used in the projects whether explicitly or implicitly, and about why we must create and value collaborative spaces where we can grow as a collective of leaders beyond specific projects. We have also furthered our understanding of what culture change means in the contexts in which we each work, and therefore what parts of this culture we are interested in changing, whether related to civically engaged scholarship or not. I have heard several times from my colleagues that the collaborative spaces I create are very counterculture and therefore themselves a way to create culture change.

It is also evident that the pandemic, the anti-racist movement, and the recent climate change–related events in various parts of the world such as wildfires, floods, and extreme heat were very much present in our minds through this reflective dialogical, collaborative-writing process. While not all wrote about all the themes that guided our conversations, everyone wrote about the pandemic and the anti-racist movement with honesty about how it affected their work and their lives, and with a sense of urgency about being part of creating a more just world.

We all resonate with the possibility that the time we spent doing just about everything from our homes gave us time to pause and reflect on our present roles in creating the world we have and our future roles in creating the world we would like to have. This isolation also forced us to pay attention to the Black Live Matters demonstrations in the streets of the United States and in many other countries in the summer of 2020, in ways we perhaps would not have done in a pre-pandemic context when we all had multiple activities and things to attend to. Yet, as more of us in the United States began to have access to vaccination and life outside our homes became busier, I sense that this reflective, attentive window is at risk of closing. Hopefully not completely, and not immediately.

The Black Live Matters movement in the United States inspired progress toward racial equity in several cities by shifting their budgetary priorities toward less policing and more social services, particularly in 2020 and 2021, including Los Angeles and New York. The political pendulum is always moving, however, and there will always be new and competing priorities, such as, for example, the Russian invasion of Ukraine and the multiple mass shootings (unrelated to police brutality) we have continued to witness in this country. These and other events have decreased the focus on racial equity. Yet for many of us there is still a sense that racial equity is experiencing a new historical moment and that the window of opportunity is still open. For example, we celebrate the many more African Americans and other marginalized groups we are seeing in Hollywood and on television, and the multiple celebrations throughout the country about Juneteenth becoming a national holiday in 2021 clearly give us reason to be optimistic. But we have also seen the growth of a strong movement for white supremacy and conservative values and a rise in specific hate crimes against nonwhite groups, more notable since Donald Trump was elected US president.

None of this discourages me from pursuing my commitment to playing a role in protecting the gains we have made and to continue working for more collaborative, democratic spaces in our institutions and communities, each in our own ways, and hopefully collectively. In a way, through our reflective, collaborative writing, we have begun a small but focused movement to be intentional about creating more collaborative spaces where we can replicate what we did in the five projects: learning, acting, and building collective leadership to create more humane, collaborative, just institutions and communities.

Our democratic society has been fragmented for a long time, causing advocates and organizers to also work in fragmented ways; all of us are competing against each other for resources, each of us choosing social problems we want to work on, often disconnected from each other. Building collaborative spaces such as the five projects has become my way to counter this democratic fragmentation, one collaborative space at a time, but always hoping those participating in these spaces will take this way of working and being and spread it to other spaces where they work and exist. All of my writing partners seem energized to do so. Hopefully those reading this book will be energized as well. In IAF organizing terms, this is called replicating myself.

Writing this book in a reflective, collaborative format has proven to be quite a rewarding learning experience, but it has also been challenging for a number of reasons. For starters, it was the first time I attempted writing this way, and the first time doing anything usually comes with growing pains. I went into this writing approach wanting to include the voices, through their own writing and authoring, of those who were participants in my research-in-action projects. It has always troubled me that we as academics tend to write "about" and not "with" our research participants. Figuring out how to balance how much feedback and direction to give my co-authors and being supportive without controlling what they wrote about their experiences in the projects was a source of learning, but also of much tension. I had tried using long, direct quotations in previous publications, but I still had full control of the writing. In addition, as the authors of chapter 7 put it so eloquently, this way of writing "requires more emotional space than traditional academic or professional writing."

Given the lessons I have learned, I can now comfortably use this writing format, and I can openly name community organizing, research in action, and narrative inquiry as democratic, action-oriented methodologies. To bring back the inspirational quote at the beginning of this chapter, I believe that the transformation of our society is possible, and it is necessary for the survival of all people and the planet. Let us work together toward redefining humanity through our own individual and collective transformation, in relationship with each other and with the land.

Notes

1. Charlene A. Carruthers, *Unapologetic: A Black, Queer, and Feminist Mandate for Radical Movements* (Boston: Beacon Press, 2019).
2. The concept of funds of knowledge comes from Norma González, Luis C. Moll, and Cathy Amanti, *Funds of Knowledge: Theorizing Practices in Households, Communities, and Classrooms* (New York: Routledge, 2005).

Afterword

The challenges of the overlapping crises of COVID-19 and the resulting economic fallout, climate destruction, and long-overdue racial reckoning have shone a light on the fractured and unhealthy relationships between people and the institutions that govern their lives. At a time when distrust of institutions is at an all-time high among people on both the Left and Right, as demonstrated by the January 6, 2021, insurrection at the US Capitol and ongoing actions seeking the abolition of police, the collection of voices and experiences from professionals from different sectors captured in this book provide a glimpse of one possible path ahead.

By detailing their specific goals, interests, and strategies, Maria Avila and her coauthors provide valuable insights for readers who are working to transform power relations within organizations and communities, for those who find themselves questioning the status quo, and those who are looking for coconspirators to create institutions and communities where everyone can thrive. What the narratives also provide is a sense of the commitment of time and other resources, along with tools and strategies, that it takes to build a trusting community to do this work together. Perhaps most importantly, the reader gets a taste of the satisfaction and joy that is also part of the journey, which can inspire or strengthen our faith in what we can accomplish collectively.

In chapter 1 and in the conclusion, Maria tells us that the key question she asked of herself and her coauthors is whether their work together toward building collective leadership has indeed created culture change. We read the answers from her coauthors throughout their respective chapters. In chapter 4, Aixle Aman Rivera and Ray López-Chang, writing from their experience as members of a school board district office, describe how the culture of their office changed from a culture where the staff saw their jobs as serving their constituents to a culture of building deep, trusting relationships with their constituents, while teaching them the skills to organize their own communities. Building the skills of a group of community-engaged professionals to examine their aspirations for their workplaces, their communities, and our world is an incredibly important body of work. Creating the capacity for people to connect meaningfully with others, find deeper meaning in their work, and take tangible steps toward creating the world in which they want to live is a valuable end in itself.

In chapter 3, writing from an academic perspective, Enrique Ortega provides a powerful description of how engaging in collective leadership has benefited him as an individual. He writes, "Sharing my narrative and intentionally practicing my profession with civic and democratic actions can help me bridge different aspects of my life into a common effort that is coherent" and provides a foundation for his "purposeful career in public health." This level of clarity about and integration of the personal and public aspects of a person's life not only serves to sustain a leader emotionally and professionally but also provides an example for anyone looking to find meaning and make a contribution to the world, aspirations that are particularly important to nonprofit workers and young people just starting their careers in any sector. I know this because I have worked with elected officials, in higher education, and in the nonprofit sector for over two decades, and I have had the opportunity to work with and mentor many professionals in all these sectors.

Reading through the chapters, we also learn that the narrative inquiry process that was foundational to the creation of this book allowed the coauthors to continue with the process of discernment about their own stories, values, and lived experiences that is part of defining self-interest in the community organizing model and which is so important to creating personal and collective resilience in the face of institutional and societal challenges. That these lessons emerged from the experiences of people who hold varying professional roles, work in diverging academic disciplines, from diverse racial/ethnic and class backgrounds testifies to the power that this kind of relational work has to bridge the divisions that might keep us from seeing each other as kin and joining together to activate our power to recreate our institutions in alignment with our hopes and dreams. This model of collective leadership also holds promise for creating more equitable and inclusive organizations, an espoused goal of many institutions in the wake of the racial reckoning of recent years. We get this sense from the coauthors of chapter 5, as they reveal how working relationally disrupts traditional power dynamics. They state: "Hierarchies tend to magnify the faults of those at the top and stifle the contributions of those at the bottom. With horizontal collective leadership we are free to teach and learn from each other according to our abilities and our needs." Since we know that people from groups that have been historically marginalized are very often excluded from holding positional power, the relational way of working is an important tool for creating the conditions for leaders from all backgrounds to activate their power and create change.

This disruption of traditional hierarchy, along with the trust-building and hope-giving aspects of the community organizing approach, have had a deep and long-lasting impact in my own life. They have helped me articulate my purpose as a young civically engaged first-generation white-collar professional and sustained me as I have advanced through a career that has taken me from higher education to work with nonprofit organizations focused on educational equity, leadership development, and capacity building for nonprofit organizations and networks working for systems change.

My first exposure to the community organizing methods used as the foundation for all the projects described here came when I was mentored by Maria Avila as a staff member at the Center for Community Based Learning (CCBL) at Occidental College. An eager and successful student for most of my life, I had left graduate school with deep feelings of disappointment and burning questions related to how and why the structures of higher education in the United States seemed to willfully ignore the contributions and concerns of working-class communities of color like the ones where I had been raised. I was also carrying a profound, but hidden, mistrust of institutional power, inherited from my Chicanx and Pueblo ancestors who had experienced discrimination and exclusion over many decades. I had not yet put these emotions into words when I started working alongside Maria, Occidental faculty and students, and community members to transform the relationship between Occidental and the surrounding community. It was through the organizing process that I was able to reflect on my experiences and began to understand that the struggles I had faced as a first-generation college student were not individual failures resulting from personal deficits but symptoms of an academic culture whose values and structures made it difficult for a person with my cultural values to succeed. I also began to unpack the underlying skepticism (sometimes cynicism) that came out of the distrust of institutions I had inherited from my ancestors. My participation in community organizing at CCBL helped me bring a more engaged, more hopeful stance to my work and exposed me to a way of working for change that felt much more sustainable and impactful than the models of community action I had seen elsewhere.

Since that time, I have used the organizing tools I learned in every professional role I have had and have passed them along to colleagues and those I coach and mentor. I offer one example to illustrate. In the spring of 2020, I had the privilege of using my skills working on a team of consultants and community residents that cocreated a bilingual (English-Spanish) leadership development curriculum for community residents from marginalized communities in Southern California. The sense of purpose, mutual learning, and power sharing that came out of our relational way of working together was the best antidote to the physical isolation and sense of despair caused by the pandemic and other upheavals of 2020. Being involved in the creation of this book, and in conversation with its cocreators, was another source of hope in a dark and confusing time.

The breadth of projects described here, along with the interweaving of individual narratives that touch on the coauthors' experiences as whole human beings with family histories, individual struggles, hopes and dreams, make a compelling and informative text that invites the reader to go deeper into their own self-reflection. For this reason, I fully expect that for many practitioners working for social change in higher education, philanthropy, government, community-based organizations, and other fields, this book will take its place alongside the work of strategists and thinkers like Marshall Ganz, adrienne maree brown, Patrice Cullors, Margaret Wheatley, Brené Brown, and others who are putting forward new frameworks and ways of being and doing our collective work to create the world as it should be. This moment calls for nothing less.

Alexis Moreno, Senior Strategist, Center for Nonprofit Management

Glossary of Terms and Concepts

action As used in this book, an organizing related action is a collectively planned, time-limited, and intentional effort designed to achieve a certain goal.

agitation This refers to provoking emotional and conceptual insight through probing questions or challenging information. Agitation shifts prior beliefs and helps us form hypotheses about possibilities for chan ge.

civic engagement, community engagement, and service learning (CE/SL) These are terms used in this book to refer to different ways in which higher education and community organizations partner.

collective impact As used in this book, collective impact is viewed as a framework by which a cross-section of civic leaders collaborate to solve a shared problem focused on equity to ultimately achieve sustainable and transformative change in communities.

collective power A type of power described in this book that is made possible when individuals are united around a shared goal. Unlike positional power, collective power can be described as "power *with*" because this power is strengthened when it is shared with others.

critical reflection We use this term to describe an organizing practice that asks organizers to regularly assess situations and their learnings objectively and to digest thoughts and ideas, especially during one-on-one meetings. It also refers to individual reflection in response to agitation and to collective reflection in order to learn from actions.

crowdsourcing This term refers to a new form of work when a crowdsourcer (organization or individual) broadcasts open calls to the crowd registered on an online digital platform (i.e., Amazon Mechanical Turk) to tap into the large-scale, on-demand virtual labor force to complete micro-tasks that are difficult to automate.

culture change This term is used in this book to refer to *changing* the parts of cultures in our institutions, communities, and organizations that aim to divide rather than foster collaboration and to make unilateral decisions rather than collaborative ones; the goal is to cocreate collaborative spaces where democratic values and practices are enhanced.

ethnographic service learning As used in this book, this term connects ethnography with service learning pedagogy, and by doing so it highlights the integration of the humanistic and scientific sides of anthropology.

Family Problem Solving Group (FPSG) A framework that the Los Angeles Unified School District Board District 5 team adapted from the Center for Public Research and Leadership's framework at Columbia University. The Board District 5 process asked constituents to identify a problem they wanted to improve in their school communities, perform a root cause analysis on that problem, and brainstorm solutions they would implement to solve it.

high-impact educational practices (HIPs) A set of pedagogical strategies used in higher education to improve student success as measured by retention and graduation rates. Examples include student research experiences, writing-intensive courses, service learning/internships, global learning/study abroad, learning communities, and collaborative activities.

house meeting A term used in this book to describe a gathering of individuals to surface issues they care deeply about. Organizers use this organizing practice to identify shared interests among those in attendance.

Industrial Areas Foundation (IAF) This is an international organizing network founded by the late Saul Alinsky in 1940 in Chicago.

narrative inquiry As used in this book, it refers to learning through sharing of personal and professional stories that evolved in the context of the collaborative, cocreative process of research in action.

one-on-ones See *relational meetings*.

Parent Action Workshop A workshop developed by the Los Angeles Unified School District Board District 5 team to introduce parents to various organizing practices.

positional power A type of power described in this book that is derived from an individual's title or position. This type of power allows the individual to have power *over* others as a result of this position.

positionality This term refers to the idea that our personal narratives, values, and experiences shape how we see and understand the world.

power analysis This is the systematic analysis of power relevant to an organizational goal for the purpose of developing effective tactics to achieve that goal.

relational meetings This term is used in this book to describe informal conversations with strategic and calculated goals of uncovering each individual's self-interests.

research in action Research in action is used in this book to highlight that in all five projects shared here, every aspect of research design and resulting actions evolved through a cocreative and collaborative process between researcher/organizer and participants, rather than through a specific purpose and research question/s defined from the start of the projects.

self-interest A term used in this book to describe what an individual cares about and why. Self-interests can be represented by how individuals spend their time, energy, money; who they connect with and can call on at any given moment; what institutions they are part of; and what they value.

transactional A term we use to distinguish between relationships where all involved parties are part of cocreating a partnership that is reciprocal and mutually beneficial, and relationships that are contractual in nature and where each party aims to gain as much as possible, such as in a sales transaction.

Bibliography

Anderson, Dick, ed. "Springing into Action: Conversation Replaces Confrontation as the College Re-examines Its Commitment to Racial Equality and a Host of Other Hot-Button Issues." *Occidental Magazine*, Spring 2019. https://www.oxy.edu/magazine/issues/spring-2019/springing-action.

Avila, Maria. "Reflecting on and Sharing Our Stories Can Transform Society." In *Asset-Based Community Engagement in Higher Education*, edited by John Hamerlinck and Julie Plaut, 17–30. Minneapolis: Minnesota Campus Compact, 2014.

Avila, Maria. *Transformative Civic Engagement through Community Organizing*. Sterling, VA: Stylus, 2018.

Avila, Maria, Adriana Aldana, and Michelle Zaragoza. "The Use of Counternarratives in a Social Work Course from a Critical Race Theory Perspective." In *Routledge Handbook of Counter-Narratives*, edited by Klarissa Lueg and Marianne Wolff Lundholt, 255–66. London: Routledge, 2020.

Beck, Sam. "Community Service Learning: A Model for Teaching and Activism." *North American Dialog* 9 (2006): 1–7.

Bouligny III, Edgar. "The Allure of the Watts Rebellion." *Toro Historical Review* 10, no. 1 (2021): 55–77.

Brown, Adrienne Maree. *Emergent Strategy: Shaping Change, Changing World*. Chico, CA: AK Press, 2017.

Burton, John K., and Paul F. Merrill. "Needs Assessment: Goals, Needs, and Priorities." In *Instructional Design Principles and Applications*, 2nd ed., edited by Leslie J. Briggs, Kent L. Gustafson, and Murray H. Tillman, 17–43. Englewood Cliffs, NJ: Educational Technology Publications, 1991.

Carruthers, Charlene A. *Unapologetic: A Black, Queer, and Feminist Mandate for Radical Movements*. Boston: Beacon, 2019.

Castillo, Celestina. "Building a Regional Cluster for Cultural Change in Higher Education: The Imagining America SoCal Cluster." Imagining

America, September 2020. https://imaginingamerica.org/wp-content/uploads/IA-SoCal-Cluster-Regional-Organizing-Paper.pdf.

Cholewa, Blaire, Rachael D. Goodman, Cirecie West-Olatunji, and Ellen Amatea. "A Qualitative Examination of the Impact of Culturally Responsive Educational Practices on the Psychological Well-Being of Students of Color." *Urban Review* 46 (2014): 574–96.

Clandinin, Jean, and Janice Huber. "Narrative Inquiry." In *International Encyclopedia of Education*, 3rd ed., edited by Barry McGaw, Eva Baker, and Penelope L. Peterson. New York: Elsevier, in press.

Deng, Xuefei (Nancy), K. D. Joshi, and Robert D. Galliers. "The Duality of Empowerment and Marginalization in Microtask Crowdsourcing: Giving Voice to the Less Powerful through Value Sensitive Design." *MIS Quarterly* 42, no. 2 (2016): 279–302.

DiAngelo, Robin J. *White Fragility: Why It's So Hard for White People to Talk about Racism*. Boston: Beacon, 2018.

Fairhurst, Gail T., Brad Jackson, Erica G. Foldy, and Sonia M. Ospina. "Studying Collective Leadership: The Road Ahead." *Human Relations* 73, no. 4 (2020): 598–614.

Freire, Paulo. *Pedagogy of the Oppressed*. New York: Continuum, 1995.

Gale, Ken, and Jonathan Wyatt. "Working at the Wonder: Collaborative Writing as Method of Inquiry." *Qualitative Inquiry* 23, no. 5 (2016): 355–64.

Ganz, Marshall. "Public Narrative, Collective Action, and Power." In *Accountability through Public Opinion: From Inertia to Public Action*, edited by Sina Odugbemi and Taeku Lee, 273–89. Washington, DC: World Bank, 2011.

Gay, Geneva. *Culturally Responsive Teaching: Theory, Research, and Practice*. New York: Teachers College Press, 2000.

González, Norma, Luis C. Moll, and Cathy Amanti. *Funds of Knowledge: Theorizing Practices in Households, Communities, and Classrooms*. New York: Routledge, 2005.

Graham, Mekada J. *Reflective Thinking in Social Work: Learning from Student Narratives*. New York: Routledge, 2017.

Hanson, Cindy, Chantelle Renwick, José Sousa, and Angelina Weenie. "Decolonizing and Indigenizing Adult Education." In *Proceedings of the 37th CASAE/ACÉÉA Annual Conference*, edited by Robert McGray and Vera Woloshyn, 98–103. Regina, SK: University of Regina, 2018.

hooks, bell, and Cornel West. *Breaking Bread: Insurgent Black Intellectual Life*. Boston: South End Press, 1991.

Horton, Myles, and Paulo Freire. *We Make the Road by Walking: Conversations on Education and Social Change*. Edited by Brenda Bell, John Gaventa, and John Peters. Philadelphia: Temple University Press, 1990.

Howe, Jeff. "The Rise of Crowdsourcing." *Wired*, June 1, 2006, 1–4.
Hurston, Zora Neale. *Barracoon: The Story of the Last "Black Cargo."* New York: Amistad, 2018.
Institute of Medicine (US) Committee on Health Care in America. "Building Organizational Supports for Change." In *Crossing the Quality Chasm: A New Health System for the 21st Century,* 111–44. Washington, DC: National Academies Press, 2001. https://www.ncbi.nlm.nih.gov/books/NBK222276/.
Ivey, Jean. "Service Learning Research." *Pediatric Nursing* 37, no. 2 (2011): 74–76.
James, Melanie. "Emergent Strategy." In *The International Encyclopedia of Strategic Communication,* edited by Robert L. Heath, Winni Johansen, Jesper Falkheimer, Kirk Hallahan, Juliana J. C. Raupp, and Benita Steyn. Hoboken, NJ: John Wiley & Sons, 2018.
Kollowich, Steve. "Blasting Academic Silos: American University Officials Say the Insularity of Colleges within Universities Is a Bane to Both I.T. Efficiency and Scholarly Innovation." *Inside Higher Ed*, January 18, 2010. https://www.insidehighered.com/news/2010/01/18/blasting-academic-silos.
Kuh, George, Ken O'Donnell, and Carol Geary Schneider. "HIPs at Ten." *Change: The Magazine of Higher Learning* 49, no. 5 (2017): 8–16.
Medeiros, Melanie A., and Jennifer Guzmán. "Ethnographic Service Learning: An Approach for Transformational Learning." *Teaching Anthropology* 6 (2016): 66–72.
McIntyre, Alice. *Participatory Action Research.* Thousand Oaks, CA: SAGE, 2008.
Mills, C. Wright. *Sociological Imagination.* New York: Oxford University Press, 2000.
Occidental College. "Springing into Action: Conversation Replaces Confrontation as the College Re-examines Its Commitment to Racial Equality and a Host of Other Hot-Button Issues." *Occidental College Magazine*, June 5, 2019, https://www.oxy.edu/magazine/issues/spring-2019/springing-action.
O'Meara, KerryAnn. *Because I Can: Exploring Faculty Civic Agency.* Kettering Foundation Working Paper 2012–1. Accessed August 16, 2021. https://www.kettering.org/sites/default/files/product-downloads/OMeara-KFWP2012-01-FINAL.pdf.
O'Meara, KerryAnn. "Encouraging Multiple Forms in Faculty Reward Systems: Does It Make a Difference?" *Research in Higher Education* 46, no. 5 (2005): 479–510.
Patterson, Gerrelyn. "A Historically Black High School Remains Intact: We Weren't Thinking about White Students." In *School Desegregation*, edited by George W. Noblit, 63–78. Boston: Sense, 2015.

Peters, Scott J. *Democracy and Higher Education: Traditions and Stories of Civic Engagement.* East Lansing: Michigan State University Press, 2010.

Ranson, Kelly and Lauren Outland. "Improving Glycemic Control among Incarcerated Men." *GSTF Journal of Nursing and Health Care* 3, no.1 (November 2015): 58–61.

Ribera, Amy K., Angie L. Miller, and Amber D. Dumford. "Sense of Peer Belonging and Institutional Acceptance in the First Year: The Role of High-Impact Practices." *Journal of College Student Development* 58, no. 4 (2017): 545–63.

Rosas, Ana Elizabeth. "Undocumented Emotional Intelligence: Learning from the Intellectual Investment of California's Undergraduates." *Boom California* (blog), December 07, 2017, https://boomcalifornia.org/2017/12/07/undocumented-emotional-intelligence/.

Sanday, Peggy Reeves, and Karl Jannowitz. "Public Interest Anthropology: A Boasian Service-Learning Initiative." *Michigan Journal of Community Service Learning* 10, no. 3 (2004): 64–75.

Snyder-Hall, Claire. *Civic Aspirations: Why Some Higher Education Faculty Are Reconnecting Their Professional and Public Lives.* Dayton, OH: Kettering Foundation, 2013.

Spiller, Chellie, Rachel Maunganui Wolfgramm, Ella Henry, and Robert Pouwhare. "Paradigm Warriors: Advancing a Radical Ecosystems View of Collective Leadership from an Indigenous Māori Perspective." *Human Relations* 73, no. 4 (2019): 516–43.

Stoecker, Randy, and Elizabeth Tryon. *The Unheard Voices: Community Organizations and Service Learning.* Philadelphia: Temple University Press, 2009.

Taylor, Sarah. *On Being Maya and Getting By: Heritage Politics and Community Development in Yucatán.* Boulder: University Press of Colorado, 2018.

Warren, Mark R., and Karen L. Mapp. *A Match on Dry Grass: Community Organizing as a Catalyst for School Reform.* New York: Oxford University Press, Inc., 2011.

Wheeler, Jen. "CLASS Coalition Demands a Voice to Ensure Equity for Vulnerable Students and Families." *United Way Greater Los Angeles* (blog), June 23, 2020. https://www.unitedwayla.org/en/news-resources/blog/class-coalition-demands-voice-ensure-equity-vulnerable-students-and-families/.

White, Byron. *Navigating the Power Dynamics between Institutions and Their Communities.* Kettering Foundation, 2009. Accessed August 16, 2021. https://www.kettering.org/sites/default/files/product-downloads/Navigating_Power_Dynamics.pdf.

Index

academia, collective leadership and relational organizing in. *See* collective leadership and relational organizing
Academic Senate, 42n5
action, concept of, 5, 12, 14–16, 19, 25, 32–33, 162, 191
agitation, as organizing skill, 68, 74–75, 100, 191
Aixle. *See* Rivera, Aixle Aman
Alan. *See* Knoerr, Alan P.
Algebra Project, 99, 100, 106
Amazon, 148
Amazon Mechanical Turk, 191
anthropology, as academic discipline, 133–34
anti-racist movement, xi, 3, 23, 24, 39, 181–83, 185; civically engaged disciplines interacting with larger community and, 52, 53–54; culture change and, 179–81; IA FLC and, 114, 129–34, 179–80; IA Southern California regional cluster and, 107, 167; integrating civic engagement into general education curriculum and, 151–52, 155, 180
APLA Health, 123
Avila, Maria, ix–xii, 1, 6–13, 16–17, 29, 35, 160, 185, 188; civically engaged disciplines project and, 44, 46, 47; IA FLC and, 112–13, 118; IA Southern California regional cluster and, 83–85, 91, 92, 93–94, 99, 107, 168–70; integrating civic engagement into general education curriculum and, 138–42; school board district team project and, 63, 71

Barbosa, Gabriella, 77
Barracoon: The Story of the Last "Black Cargo" (Hurston), 133–34
BD 5 (Los Angeles Unified School District, Board District 5). *See* school board district team, creating community organizing culture in
bilingual leadership development curriculum, 189
BIPOC (Black, Indigenous, and People of Color). *See* anti-racist movement; diversity and people of color
Black Lives Matter. *See* anti-racist movement
Boyle Heights Museum (BHM), 100–101, 166
Breaking Bread (hooks and West), 39
Bringing Theory to Practice (BT2P), 139, 140, 158n2
Brown, Brené, 190

California Faculty Association, 42n5
California State University, Dominguez Hills (CSUDH), 26, 43, 61n4, 107, 112, 116, 117, 123, 130, 139, 141, 142,

Index

California State University, Dominguez Hills (*continued*) 144, 150–53, 159n7, 171, 173. *See also* Imagining America (IA) Faculty Learning Community (FLC); integrating civic engagement into general education curriculum
California State University, Northridge, College of the Canyons, 139
campus, collective leadership and relational organizing on. *See* collective leadership and relational organizing
Capitol insurrection (Jan. 6, 2021), 185
Carnegie Foundation, 102
Carruthers, Charlene A., 160
CASA 0101 (community theater), 101
Castillo, Celestina, 21, 83–84, 88–89, 91, 92, 94, 97–99, 102–3, 107, 166–69, 177–78
CE (civic/community engagement). *See* civic engagement
Celestina. *See* Castillo, Celestina
Center for Community Based Learning (CCBL), Occidental College, 16, 83, 84, 91, 93–94, 98, 99, 102, 105, 109, 143, 164, 188–89
Center for Conscious Creativity, 104
Center for Engagement with Los Angeles, Occidental College, 100
Center for Public Research and Leadership (CPRL), Columbia University, 77, 82
Center for Service-Learning, Internships, and Civic Engagement (SLICE), CSUDH, 112, 139–42, 144, 172–74
Central American Resource Center (CARECEN), 123
Cerritos College, 139, 140
Chai, Kathleen Tornow, 20–21, 43–61, 163–64
civic agency, 17, 34, 40, 162
civic engagement: concept of civically engaged scholarship, 29–30; defined, 191; IA FLC, creating collaborative space for civic engagement at, 113, 126–27; IA FLC, interdisciplinary collaboration and community engagement at, 118–19; models of, 18–19; related/alternative terms, 158n1, 191; SLICE, CSUDH, 112, 139–40, 141, 142, 144. *See also* civically engaged disciplines interacting with larger community; integrating civic engagement into general education curriculum
civically engaged disciplines interacting with larger community, 3, 20–21, 43–61, 186–87; assessing success of building collaborative leadership through, 163–64; collaborative space in academia, lack of, 45–48; democratic society, contribution to, 43, 44; future of collaborative leadership in, 56–61; narrative reflection and, 52–56; PAR and research in action, 51–52; professional narratives, use of, 48–51; purpose and description of project, 43, 44–45
climate change, 107, 181–82, 185
Coalition for Humane Immigrant Rights Los Angeles (CHIRLA), 123
cocreating knowledge, 37
collaborative writing, 1–5, 38–40, 155–58, 180, 183–84
collective impact, 66, 191
collective leadership and relational organizing, 6–27, 29–41, 160–84; anti-racist movement and, xi, 3, 23, 24, 39 (*see also* anti-racist movement); assessing success of, 161–74; bilingual leadership development curriculum, 189; civic agency, concept of, 17, 34, 40, 162; civic engagement models compared, 18–19; civically engaged scholarship, importance of, 29–30; collaborative writing and, 1–5, 38–40; community organizing practices compared, 19, 20; competitiveness of academic culture and, 31; COVID-19 pandemic and, xi, 3, 24, 27, 39, 41n2 (*see also* COVID-19 pandemic);

Index   201

culture change through, 24–27, 29–31, 174–81 (*see also* culture change); evaluating and assessing projects, 22–24; IAF model for developing, 14–16; indigenous communities, lessons learned from, 6–7, 17–18; individual scholarship, transitioning from, 31–33; methodological approaches, 35–41; narrative inquiry and, 37–38 (*see also* narrative inquiry); personal/academic roots of author and, 6–13, 16–17; research in action and, 35–38 (*see also* research in action); stakeholders in, 30, 33–35, 41n1; steps in, 19–20. *See also* civically engaged disciplines interacting with larger community; Imagining America (IA) Faculty Learning Community (FLC); Imagining America (IA) Southern California regional cluster; integrating civic engagement into general education curriculum; school board district team, creating community organizing culture in
collective power, 72, 74, 98, 191
Communities for Los Angeles Student Success (CLASS) Coalition, 68–69
community, definitional use of, 28n2
community engagement. *See* civic engagement
community health, civic engagement, and collaboration. *See* civically engaged disciplines interacting with larger community
community organizing practices, 19, 20
competitive academic culture, 31
COVID-19 pandemic, xi, 3, 24, 27, 39, 41n2, 181–82, 185; civically engaged disciplines interacting with larger community and, 52, 53; culture change and, 179–81; IA FLC and, 114, 129–34, 179–80; IA Southern California regional cluster and, 60, 93, 95, 105, 107, 108, 167; integrating civic engagement into general education curriculum and, 149, 151–52, 155–56, 180; school board district team, creating community organizing culture in, 69, 82
Creating Culture Change through Regional Cluster Organizing (IA webinar), 95
Cree people, 6, 7
critical reflection, 32, 70, 75–76, 86, 100, 177, 191
crowdsourcing, 147–48, 191
CSUDH. *See* California State University, Dominguez Hills (CSUDH)
Cullors, Patrice, 190
culturally responsive practices, 120
culture change, 24–27, 29–31, 174–81; assessing success of projects at, 174–79, 186; in civically engaged disciplines interacting with larger community, 56–61; COVID-19/anti-racism movement and, 179–81; defined, 192; IA FLC and, 114, 134–37; IA Southern California regional cluster and, 85, 86, 88, 92, 93, 95–106, 107–10, 168, 169, 177–78; imagining and practicing, 95–100; institutional cultures, 100–106; integrating civic engagement into general education curriculum and, 151–55; school board district team, creating community organizing culture in, 64, 65, 69–71, 74, 79, 81, 175–77; time required for, 108–10

Deferred Action for Childhood Arrivals (DACA), 129
Deng, Xuefei (Nancy), 22, 138, 140, 142–43, 147–49, 152–53, 171–73, 180
diabetes, prison inmates with, 51
DiAngelo, Robin, 54
diversity and people of color, x, 2, 53–54, 98, 110, 130, 131. *See also* anti-racist movement

202 Index

elected school board. *See* school board district team, creating community organizing culture in Enrique. *See* Ortega, Enrique
Espiritu de Nuestro Futuro (ENF), 123
ethnographic service learning: CSUDH program, 123–26; defined, 192

faculty handbook at Occidental College, revising, 102–3, 10110
Faculty Learning Communities (FLCs): IA FLC at CSUDH (*see* Imagining America [IA] Faculty Learning Community [FLC]); integrating civic engagement FLC at CSUDH, 139–40, 144, 153 (*see also* integrating civic engagement into general education curriculum)
Family Problem Solving Groups (FPSGs), 76, 77–78, 79, 81, 192
First-Generation Program committee, 132
FLC. *See* Faculty Learning Communities (FLCs)
Floyd, George, murder of, 53, 107, 151. *See also* anti-racist movement
FPSGs. *See* Family Problem Solving Groups (FPSGs)
Freire, Paulo, 39
funds of knowledge, 114, 120, 127, 136, 170, 184n2

Gabbie. *See* Seiwert, Gabrielle
Gale, Ken, 38–39
Ganz, Marshall, 33, 190
general education, integrating civic engagement with. *See* integrating civic engagement into general education curriculum
George. *See* Sánchez, George J.
Graham, Mekada, 33
Great Public Schools Now, 69
grocery store, organizing campaign for, South Central Los Angeles, 10–13
Guzmán, Jennifer, 125

handbook for Occidental College faculty, revising, 102–3, 10110
Hanson, Cindy, 6
health services, civic engagement, and collaboration. *See* civically engaged disciplines interacting with larger community
Henry, Ella, 17, 37
high-impact [educational] practices (HIPs), 120, 141, 147, 158n3, 192
hooks, bell, 39
Horton, Mike, 39
house meetings, 73–74, 192
Hurston, Zora Neale, 133–34

IA. *See* Imagining America (IA)
IAF. *See* Industrial Areas Foundation (IAF)
Imagining America (IA), 85, 113
Imagining America (IA) Faculty Learning Community (FLC), 2–3, 21, 112–37; assessing success of building collaborative leadership through, 170–71; collaborative space for civic engagement, creating, 113, 126–27; culture change and, 114, 134–37; description of project, 113–14; ethnographic service learning program, 123–26; immigrant photo essays and community exhibit, 120–23; interdisciplinary collaboration and community engagement at, 118–19; narrative inquiry, utility of, 113, 114–18, 119, 127–28; research in action at, 113, 119; trust, creating, 113–14
Imagining America (IA) Southern California regional cluster, 2, 21, 83–110; assessing success of building collaborative leadership through, 166–70, 187–88; benefits of membership in, 87; connecting local communities and academic institutions, 90–92; culture change and, 85, 86, 88, 92, 93, 95–106, 107–10, 168, 169, 177–78; description

of project, 85–86; evolution of, 106–8; imagining and practicing culture change, 95–100; institutional cultures, changing, 100–106; Joy of Giving Something Fellowship, 87; mentoring at, 106; narrative inquiry at, 88–90, 96–106; organizing practices, cluster structure emerging from, 92–95; PAGE Fellows program, 87; time needed for culture change, commitment to, 108–10; unity and diversity, interplay between, 110
Imelda (pseud.), 15–16
Immigrant Student Alliance, 123
immigrants and immigration, ix, 10, 11, 15, 65, 67, 88, 90, 112, 115, 116, 120–23, 129–32, 165, 168, 170
indigenous communities, 6–7, 17–18, 37, 117–18, 133, 134, 168, 170
Industrial Areas Foundation (IAF), 8–10, 12–14, 16, 28n3, 62, 99, 162–63, 183, 192
Institute of Medicine, 57
institutions: culture change at, 100–106; definitional use of, 28n2; high-level societal distrust of, 185
integrating civic engagement into general education curriculum, 3, 21–22, 138–58; assessing success of building collaborative leadership through, 171–74; collaborative writing and, 155–58; collective leadership model used for, 144–51; culture change and, 151–55; description of project, 139–40; FLC and, 139–40, 144, 153; narrative inquiry and, 140–44

Joanna. See Perez, Joanna B.
Joint Educational Project (JEP), USC, 104
Joy of Giving Something Fellowship, IA, 87
Juneteenth, 183

Kathy. See Chai, Kathleen Tornow
Kettering Foundation, 43

Kêytê-aya, 6
Knoerr, Alan P., 21, 83, 89–93, 99–100, 102, 105–7, 166–69, 177–78

Labor Center, UCLA, 116
Leadership for Educational Equity (LEE), 66, 67, 82n3
Lopez, Josefina, 101
López-Chang, Ray, 21, 62–63, 67–69, 74, 75, 164–65, 175–77, 186
Los Angeles Neighborhood Council, 62, 82n1
Los Angeles Unified School District (LAUSD), Board District 5 (BD 5). See school board district team, creating community organizing culture in

Management Information Systems (MIS) Quarterly, 148
Maria. See Avila, Maria
math as social justice issue, 3, 83, 91–92, 99–100, 106, 177–78
McIntyre, Alice, 37
McNair Scholars Program, 131
Mead, Margaret, 133
Medeiros, Melanie A., 125
Mexican American Opportunity Foundation (MAOF), 123
Moreno, Alexis, 185–90

Nancy. See Deng, Xuefei (Nancy)
narrative inquiry, 37–38; assessing value of, 187–88; culture change, imagining and practicing, 96–100; defined, 192; at IA FLC, 113, 114–18, 119, 127–28; at IA Southern California regional cluster, 88–90, 96–106; institutional culture, changing, 100–106; integrating civic engagement into general education curriculum and, 140–44; narrative reflection, value of, 52–56; personal/academic roots of author, 6–13, 16–17; positionality and, 114; professional narratives, use of, 48–51; research in action and,

Index

narrative inquiry (*continued*)
37–38, 192; school board district team, creating community organizing culture in, 64–69, 80–81
needs assessment, 125–26
non-tenure track faculty, 34, 42n5, 100, 106
Northeast Los Angeles Education Strategy Group (ESG), 99, 105
nursing, civic engagement, and collaboration. *See* civically engaged disciplines interacting with larger community

obesity management at Samoan community health agency, 51–52
Occidental College, 35, 62, 83–84, 91, 94, 99, 100, 103, 105, 107, 109, 139, 143, 177, 188. *See also* Center for Community Based Learning (CCBL), Occidental College; Imagining America (IA) Southern California regional cluster
O'Meara, KerryAnn, 17
On Being Mayan and Getting By (Taylor), 37–38
One-LA, 99
one-on-ones (relational meetings), 71–74, 100, 193
Ortega, Enrique, 20–21, 43–61, 153–64, 186

PAGE. *See* Publicly Active Graduate Education (PAGE) Fellows program, IA
PAR. *See* participatory action research (PAR)
Parent Action Workshops (PAWs), 76–77, 78, 79, 81, 192
participatory action research (PAR), 36, 51. *See also* research in action
PAWs. *See* Parent Action Workshops (PAWs)
Perez, Joanna B., 21, 112, 114–17, 120–23, 126–32, 135–36, 138, 170–71, 179–80

personal narrative. *See* narrative inquiry
Peters, Scott, 33
Philip. *See* Vieira, Philip A.
POC (people of color). *See* anti-racist movement; diversity and people of color
positional power, 65, 66, 74, 187, 191, 192
positionality, 114, 118, 127, 130, 134, 136, 170, 192
Pouwhare, Robert, 17, 37
power, collective, 72, 74, 98, 191
power, positional, 65, 66, 74, 187, 191, 192
power analysis, 74, 100, 192
presidential election (2020), 129, 167, 179–81
prison inmates with diabetes, 51
Publicly Active Graduate Education (PAGE) Fellows program, IA, 87

Ray. *See* López-Chang, Ray
relational meetings (one-on-ones), 71–74, 100, 193
relational organizing. *See* collective leadership and relational organizing
Renwick, Chantelle, 6
research in action, 35–38; assessing success of, 162, 169, 184; Avila's practice of, xi; in civically engaged disciplines interacting with larger community, 44, 51–52; collaborative writing and, 1; collective leadership/relational organizing and, 9, 19, 20, 23, 26, 35–39; defined, 193; IA FLC and, 113, 119; integrating civic engagement into general education curriculum, 139, 140, 141, 143, 154; narrative inquiry and, 37–38, 192; PAR, as element of, 36–37
Rissi. *See* Zimmermann, Rissi
Rivera, Aixle Aman, 21, 62, 64–67, 70, 74, 164–65, 175–77, 186
Rodriguez, Ref, 65, 71, 164–65
Rosas, Ana Elizabeth, 33

Index   205

Samoan community health agency, obesity management at, 51–52
Sánchez, George J., xii, 21, 83–85, 88, 89, 91–94, 96, 100–101, 166–69, 177–78
Sarah. *See* Taylor, Sarah R.
school board district team, creating community organizing culture in, 2, 21, 62–82, 186; agitation, as organizing skill, 68, 74–75; assessing success of building collaborative leadership through, 164–65; changing from transactional to relational culture, 64, 65, 69–71, 74, 79, 81, 175–77; critical reflection, as organizing skill, 75–76; FPSGs, 76, 77–78, 79, 81, 192; fundamental organizing practices, investigating, 71–76; house meetings, 73–74; narrative inquiry, making use of, 64–69, 80–81; one-on-ones (individual relational meetings), 71–74; operationalizing and integrating organizing practices, 76–79; PAWs, 76–77, 78, 79, 81; power and power relationships, 65, 66, 72, 74; purpose and description of project, 63–64; self-interests, importance of understanding, 72, 74, 79; trust as critical foundation of, 63, 67–68, 70, 73, 75, 79–80; vulnerability, role of, 79–80, 82n8
Seiwert, Gabrielle, 22, 138, 139, 140, 142–43, 149–51, 153–54, 171–73, 180
self-interest[s], 11, 12, 19, 69, 71, 72, 74, 75, 79, 81, 187, 193
service learning (SL). *See* civic engagement
Sigma Theta Tau (nursing honor society), 59, 61n4
SLICE (Center for Service-Learning, Internships, and Civic Engagement), CSUDH, 112, 139–42, 144, 172–74
social justice, 3, 7, 43, 90, 91, 99, 106, 116–17, 130, 132–33, 154
sociology, defined, 116

Sokamba Performing Arts Company, 104–5, 107
Sousa, José, 6
Spiller, Chellie, 17, 37
Stoecker, Randy, 25
student learning outcomes (SLOs), 124–25

Tarahuma Indians, 6
Taylor, Sarah R., 21, 37–38, 112–14, 117–18, 123–26, 128, 132–34, 136, 153, 170–71, 179–80
Technology, Entertainment and Design (TEDx) conference, CSUDH, 146
Toledo, Veronica, 139, 143
Toro Dreamers Success Center, 132
transactional relationships, x, 29, 44, 48, 64, 65, 69–71, 74, 79, 81, 98, 127, 193
Transformative Civic Engagement through Community Organizing (Avila), 35
Trump, Donald, 183
trust: community organizing culture and, 63, 67–68, 70, 73, 75, 79–80; at IA FLC, 113–14; institutions, high-level societal distrust of, 185; integrating civic engagement into general education curriculum and, 149
Tryon, Elizabeth, 25

"Undocumented and Unafraid" course, CSUDH, 120–22, 130
Undocumented Student Ally Coalition (USAC), 123, 132
UndocuScholars project, 131
United Parents and Students, 143, 144, 149, 153, 154
United Way of Greater Los Angeles (UWGLA), 68–69
unity and diversity, interplay between, 110
University of Michigan, 85
University of Southern California (USC), 10, 11, 88, 91, 94, 96, 103–4, 107, 178

Vieira, Philip A., 22, 138, 140–42, 146–47, 149, 151–52, 171–73, 180
virtual world, collaborating in, 24, 54, 85, 87, 93, 105, 108, 129–32, 166–67, 170, 180
vulnerability, 79–80, 82n8

Watts Rebellion, 151, 159n7
We Make the Road by Walking (Horton and Freire), 39
"We the People" National Alliance/Math Literacy for All, 106
Weenie, Angelina, 6
West, Cornel, 39
Wheatley, Margaret, 190
White Fragility (DiAngelo), 54
White House Millennium Council, 85
white privilege, 54
white supremacy, 129, 155, 183

Wolfgramm, Maunganui, 17, 37
Woodrow Wilson National Fellowship Foundation, 85
"Working at the Wonder" (Gale and Wyatt), 38–39
writing: collaborative, 1–5, 38–40, 155–58, 180, 183–84; as inquiry, 38–40
Wyatt, Jonathan, 38–39

Xi Theta (nursing honor society), 59, 61n4
Xuefei. *See* Deng, Xuefei (Nancy)

Young People's Project, 99

Zimmermann, Rissi, 21, 83, 84, 88, 91, 92, 94, 97, 103–7, 166–69, 177–78

Ingram Content Group UK Ltd.
Milton Keynes UK
UKHW041823190323
418703UK00004BA/124